Unlock Microsoft Excel

Unlock Microsoft Excel

Volume Two of
Beyond Cut, Copy and Paste

Henry I. Balogun, Ph.D.

iUniverse, Inc.

New York   Lincoln   Shanghai

Unlock Microsoft Excel
Volume Two of Beyond Cut, Copy and Paste

iUniverse, Inc.

For information address:
iUniverse, Inc.
2021 Pine Lake Road, Suite 100
Lincoln, NE 68512
www.iuniverse.com

ISBN: 0-595-31669-7

Printed in the United States of America

To my mother—Alice Ogunmeowe Omolewa popularly known as "Iya Aladura." You did the best you could for your children with the little you had. You spent your time in obedience to your calling as a servant of God. You did not walk away from those who needed your help. And now you can truly rest in peace. Okun o èye. Suñre ó!

ACKNOWLEDGMENTS

Good friends with genuine love are not always easy to find. I'm lucky to have:
Rev. Paul Fakunle, Emmanuel Dada, Ph.D., Emeka Nwadiora, Ph.D., John
Ogunkorode, Joseph Famuyide—Attorney at Law, James L. Wells, EA, Peter
Oyeleye, Elizabeth Aliu, Susan Maria and Michel Bien-Aime, MD. I will never
forget every act of kindness and good deed done by these and many other people of goodwill that I come across daily—how they let their light shine; their
simple and down-to-earth love for the human family brings about a breath of
fresh air and a deep sense of renewed hope. I am deeply grateful to them.

CONTENTS

Making the simple complicated is commonplace; making the complicated simple, awesomely simple, that's creativity.

—Charles Mingus

INTRODUCTION

If you thought volume one of *Beyond Cut, Copy and Paste* is exiting, fun and informative, wait until you begin to experience this volume. Here we are going to focus on *Microsoft Excel* exclusively. We are going to take a careful look at the features of this powerful and extremely useful business tool. We are going to go deeper and later explore its relationship with the rest of *Microsoft Office* programs.

To fully understand computer applications, programming, or the whole process of the digital divide is to understand its concept. How many times have you hard somebody say, "You have no idea what in the universe I'm talking about, do you?" No matter how hard we try to do something, whatever it is, without proper understanding of its concept, we will always come short, time and again. Understanding concept can sometimes depend on how well rooted and grounded you are in comprehension. To fully comprehend, it is necessary to eliminate any preexisting thought likely to interfere with concentration—try as much as possible to avoid a divided attention.

A tour bus load full of noisy tourists arrives at Runnymede, England. They gather around the guide who says, "This is the spot where the barons forced King John to sign the Magna Carta."
A man pushing his way to the front of the crowd asks, "When did that happen?"
"1215," answers the guide.
The man looks at his wristwatch and says, "Shoot! Just missed it by a half hour!"

Microsoft Excel is a program popularly known as an electronic spreadsheet designed to make working with numbers (regardless of whether you are actually comfortable working with numbers or not) something to really enjoy and not something to despise. There is simply no better electronic spreadsheet, or worksheet, as some people like to refer to it.

One of the goals I hope to achieve in this volume is to remove the fear of working with numbers. To make this goal a reality, *Unlock Microsoft Excel* is hereby presented in easy to understand process. You will find how best to work with *Microsoft Excel* and produce the expected result. However, there are so many actions (as you will soon discover) that cannot be performed through point and click without the use of computer instructions, otherwise known as programming, that are capable of repeating themselves until every necessary, important, and required step is completely executed.

Chapter one entitled *Optional Configuration* is written to help you deal with some computer features that are likely to interfere with the use of your computer system. This type of help with basic configuration of the system as oppose to our subject matter, is something you will find in every volume of *Beyond Cut, Copy and Paste.* The beginning chapter is always about necessary fine-tuning of your computer system.

Before we begin to unlock *Microsoft Excel*, I'm going to take this time to introduce you to some of Excel features that may have appeared difficult to understand until now. As we go on, you will come across some similarities to *Microsoft Word* (as revealed in Volume one of *Beyond Cut, Copy and Paste)* and other members of the *Microsoft Office* group of programs. I will also call your attention to where Excel deviates from those similarities.

Entering Data in Excel

The focus of Excel is usually in the active cell and the active cell is one with the **insertion block** otherwise known as the highlight. When Excel is started, the active cell (where you will find the insertion block) is normally at the intersection of row one and column one (**A1**). You can start entering data the moment Excel is started. You can enter text as label in cases where descriptive heading is required, or use specially defined labels such as alphanumeric label. You can also enter numbers, which can be calculated using formulas. Excel is designed to recognize the type of data you enter—text, number, or formula.

Text

Excel does not treat long text the same way as *Microsoft Word*. If a text entry is too long and the cell to the right of the long text is empty, Excel continues and displays the rest of the text over the adjacent cell. But if the cell to the right of the long text contains an entry (number, text, or formula), then Excel limits the text entry to the active cell but truncate the display of the long text. To see the rest of the text, you will have to expand the active cell.

Undo, Redo and Repeat

Even though most actions can be undone, the real deal is that Excel can only reverse your last 16 actions, regardless of whether they are simple or complex. As you have seen in *Microsoft Word*, the **Redo** button reverses **Undo**. The **Edit → Repeat** lets you repeat your last action. You can use this command to repeat your last action in as many cells as you like.

Number

It is not really required to enter commas, dollar signs. The best way to handle it is to just enter the numbers and later use Excel formatting commands to add commas, dollar signs and whatever formatting is necessary and required. Always type a decimal point if the number you are entering requires one. Always type a negative number entry with a minus sign or enclose it in parenthesis.

Formulas

Formulas are equations that perform calculations on values in your worksheet. A formula starts with an equal sign (=) and does not require the use of space anywhere within the formula. Elements of formulas are as follows:

1. **Operators.** Operator is a sign, or symbol that specifies the type of calculation to perform within an expression.
2. **Constants.** Constant is a value that is not calculated and therefore does not change.
3. **Relative reference.** In a formula, the address of a cell based on the relative position of the cell that contains the formula and the cell referred to.
4. **Name.** A word or string of characters that represents a range of cells, formulas, or constant value.

Selecting Cells

There are some striking similarities to *Microsoft Word* with regard to steps required to select, or highlight texts, or numbers. You can use the mouse or the keyboard to select cells. Once cells are selected or highlighted, you can move, copy, delete or simply format as you like. However, selecting a letter or a word in a long text is not as easy in Excel as it is in Word. And when you try to select or highlight more than one cell, the first cell (the cell you started from) will look like it is on strike—like its not part of the group of cells you are trying to select. Before you start talking to yourself or yelling at your neighbor or pulling out your hair (just kidding!), I want you to know that the first cell is not being diffi-cult or rebellious—that's just the way it is suppose to appear. Nothing is wrong with your computer system or the application you are using. All I can say is wel-come to the sometimes wacky world of computer technology.

Aligning

By default, texts are aligned to the left of a cell and numbers to the right of a cell. You can always use the **Align Left, Center** or **Align Right** buttons on the toolbar to adjust as you like. Again, this is applicable to cells. You can only align within a cell or group of cells but not within an entire page as in Microsoft Word.

Other similarities to *Microsoft Word* are in the layout of their menus and tool-bars. Excel menu responds the same way to *Access Keys*. Each underlined letter works with the **Alt** key. Hold down the **Alt** key and then press any of the **Access Keys** (the underlined letter) and it will activate the pull down menu.

Excel toolbars displays screen tips just like in Microsoft Word but not along with screen shortcut. To activate screen tips, click **Tools → Customize → Option** and then click the check box next to **Show screen tips on toolbars.**

Finally, you will notice that Excel gives you a blank **workbook** in which there are three **worksheets** to begin with. You are not by any means limited to those three worksheets. You can always add more depending on your need. However, these worksheets are similar to a paper notebook which is comprised of many pages or sheets of paper.

Unlike a paper notebook, Excel comes with gridlines with horizontal rows and vertical columns. Each worksheet in Excel has 256 columns and 65,536 rows—that's an unbelievably large worksheet. The point where each row and each column meet (intersect) is known as a **cell**. For example, the point where the first row meets the first column or the second column or the third and so on and so forth is known as a **cell**. How many rows and columns are displayed at any given time depend in large measure on the size of your screen. Regardless, you can always scroll right or left, up or down to reach the rest of the rows and columns.

Introduction to this program whose name connote essence of achievement more than it does of a computer application designed to be a comprehensive business tool could go on and on, instead, let us just stop right here and begin to unfold the beauty of this incredible application.

The last chapter (presented in dialogue format) is designed to prepare you for my next book which is going to be called "*Beyond e-Mails.*" This type of conclusion is something unique to all of my series. It started from Volume One of "*Beyond Cut, Copy and Paste.*"

Microsoft, Microsoft Excel, Microsoft Word and *Microsoft PowerPoint* are the copyrighted trademarks of Microsoft Corporation.

CHAPTER ONE

Optional Configurations

Dealing with Accessibility Features

For some strange reasons, I get unsolicited e-mails everyday, and some of them are downright rude and annoying. I'm the type of person who would not mind to delete e-mails from an unrecognized source without reading them, but when I got to this one, something prompted me to read and this is what it says:

> I was at my bank to make a deposit when the clerk behind the counter turned to the computer for information. As she touched a button, a small part suddenly flew off the machine. All sorts of odd symbols started flashing across the screen. I heard her gasp, and then she turned to me in wide-eyed wonder and exclaimed, "It's swearing at me!"

I'm quite sure that this was designed to amuse its readers, but when you really look at the way most computer users handles accessibility features, don't be surprised if you sat down at your friend's computer and the system is swearing at you. How is that possible? Let's assume you inadvertently left the microphone on, and someone is really upset in the other room and yelling some inappropriate vocabularies. Believe it or not, if the microphone is turned on, and the system is in dictation mode, don't be surprised if the computer system starts displaying what the irate host is saying, word for word.

Useful Windows Shortcuts to handle accessibility features

1. To turn the microphone on or off, hold down the **Windows logo** key and press **V**.
2. To turn the handwriting feature on or off, hold down the **Windows logo** key and press **H**.
3. To switch between voice command mode and dictation mode, hold down the **Windows logo** key and press **T**.

StickyKeys

In case you have a friend, a family member, a co-worker or just an acquaintance who is having a difficult time holding down two or more keys at a time, StickyKeys is the answer. When a shortcut requires a key combination, such as **Ctrl + Alt + Del** or **Ctrl + B** for bold, or **Ctrl + P** for print, or **Ctrl + Esc** to activate Windows start menu (good for keyboards without Window logo), StickyKeys will make it possible for you to press one key at a time instead of pressing them simultaneously as is programmatically required. Always remember that the Stickykeys is there if you want to use the **Shift, Ctrl,** or **Alt** key by pressing one key at a time.

All right, no doubt about the usefulness of the **StickyKeys** but where in the universe is the **StickyKeys!** One thing you really don't want to do is try to look for it without knowing where to find it. It is not part of the keyboard keys or in a combination of keys. You simply need to call it into existence just by turning on its shortcut feature or by using the mouse to hunt for it. Let's use its shortcut feature to turn it on when we need it, or off when we don't have to use it.

To turn it on, press the **Shift** key on your keyboard **five times** and that will bring out the following popup window: (If your system does not respond to this simple command, follow the instruction on the next page.)

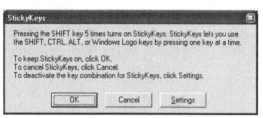

Although information on the *StickyKeys* window is self-explanatory, but there is more to it. If all you want to do is simply turn on the *StickyKeys*, you can just go ahead and click **Ok**, otherwise, click **Settings** for more choices. For now let us click **Ok**. To experience the beauty of the *Stickykeys*, press this keys (**Ctrl + Esc**, or **Ctrl + Alt + Del** [be careful not to inadvertently turn off your computer system prematurely], or try any **Shift, Ctrl,** or **Alt**) one key at a time.

To turn on StickyKeys using the mouse

1. Click the Windows **Start** button

2. Click **Setting → Control Panel.** If you are using Windows XP, click **Start → Control Panel**

3. Double click the **Accessibility Options** icon and that should bring out the following window:

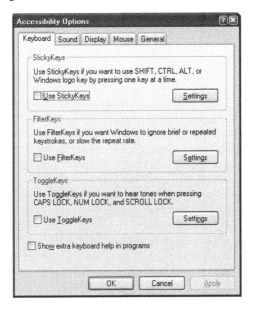

4. Click the box next to **Use StickyKeys.**

5. In addition to turning on the *Stickykeys* from the *Accessibility Options*, you can also turn on the **ToggleKeys** to add tones each time you press the **Caps Lock,** or **Num Lock,** or **Scroll Lock.** This is really neat most especially when the reading glasses are not as good as they use to be. When you hear the tone(s), you know for sure that the Cap Lock or the

Num Lock or the Scroll Lock is on. But if the reading glasses are still as effective as ever or the contact lens hasn't fall off, you might not want to be bothered with the *ToggleKeys.*

6. Click **Ok.**

> If the activation of the *StickyKeys* or the *ToggleKeys* result in conflict with the system, it is advisable to turn it off immediately and use it only when you need it.
>
> Notepad

It is not enough to do your best; you must know what to do, and then do your best.

—W. Edwards Deming

CHAPTER TWO

A Quick look at Excel Features

Starting Excel

How you start Excel or any of the programs in *Microsoft Office* depends on whether you want to open a new file or an existing file. In the case of Excel, to open a file, new or existing is to open a workbook. The process is basically the same.

To Open a New Workbook

1. Click the **Start** button, place your mouse on **Programs**, or **All Programs** (if your system is equipped with *Windows XP*) from the right pane, look for and select **Microsoft Excel,** or
2. Simply look for and click the Excel button on the *Microsoft Office Shortcut bar* from the desktop.

That should open Excel and take you to a blank worksheet in a new workbook that look like the following screenshot from Excel 2002:

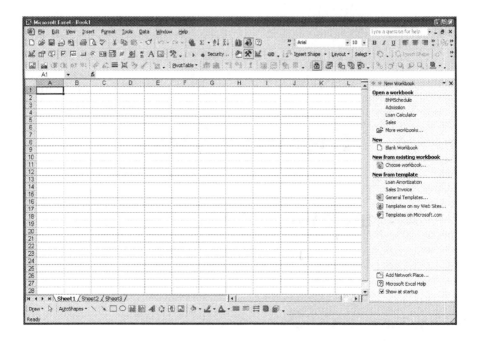

The Insertion block is in **A1**. As soon as you start typing, you will see these new toolbar buttons **×√***ƒ* showing between the **Name** box and the **Formula** bar. If you move your mouse on the **×** button, it should read **Cancel** and the next button **√** after that should read **Enter**. In Excel, after entering a text, number or formula and you press the **Enter** key on the keyboard, the Insertion block will immediately move down—below the active cell. However, after entering a text, number or formula and you click the **Enter** button on the toolbar, Excel will then perform the required action but keep the **Insertion block** at the same location.

The Name box and Formula Bar

The **Name** box and the **Formula** bar are located on the same line below the toolbars and directly on top of the grid lines and cells. The **Name** box (which is the space directly on top of the "A" column and to the left of the *Formula Bar*) usually displays the address or reference of the active cell. The following screen-shot is taken from Excel 2002, the *Name* box displays "B1" while the *Formula Bar* displays=DATEDIF(A1,TODAY(),"Y")

B1		▼	*fx* =DATEDIF(A1,TODAY(),"Y")				
	A	B	C	D	E	F	G	H
1		103						
2								

Apart from displaying cell reference, the *Name* box can be used to:

1. Move to any cell you want. For example, click the **Name** box and type **G27** and then press **Enter**. That should take the **Insertion block** to cell **G27**. This is something you will find useful in a large worksheet.

2. Name a cell or a group of cells (range). Naming cells provides a more efficient way to refer to them when they are needed in formulas, functions, etc. To name a cell or group of cells:

   a. Click the cell you want to name, or select a group of cells (range).

   b. Go to the **Name** box and type the name of the cell or group of cells.

   c. Press the **Enter** key on your keyboard.

3. To jump to a named cell or range of cells:

   a. Click the little arrow next to the Name box and this should display all the cells that are recently named

   b. Move the mouse over to the name of the cell or range you want to move to and click. Remember, you can only jump to a predefined cell or named cell.

Formula bar and formulas

The **Formula bar** simply displays the contents of the active cell. Formulas are equations that perform calculations on values in your worksheet. A formula starts with an equal sign (=) and should contain no space anywhere. For example, let's use a formula to reveal your age. Yeah, I would like to know how old you are. C'mon we are friends, right? Ok, now use the arrow key on your keyboard to move the **Insertion block** to **B1** and type this formula **=DatedIf(A1,Today(),"Y")**. You've got to type it exactly as it is, no space and do not forget to start with the equal (=) sign. Instead of using the **Enter** key on your keyboard, just click on the **Enter** button. Now take a look at the result. Does the system say you are 103 years old? Wow! Talk about rapid aging, huh? What are you going to do now that you are 103 years old? You are too old for me! Hey, don't come yelling at me, I didn't do it. Why don't you move the **Insertion block** back to **A1** using the left arrow key on your keyboard and tell the system your date of birth by typing it in this format **mm/dd/yyyy** and don't forget to click the **Enter** button, or press the **Enter** key on your keyboard. Does the system say you are 21 years old? Hey, if you are a girl, and perhaps would like to hang out at Seven Eleven or Wawa tonight, give me a call (just kidding!). Now that we both passed the compatibility test, let us examine the role of functions.

Functions

Functions are predefined formulas that perform calculations by using specific values, called arguments, in a particular order, or structure. Functions can be used to perform simple or complex calculations. For example, let us enter the following:

1. In A4, type 9 and press the Enter key on your keyboard.
2. In A5 type 20 and press the Enter key on your keyboard
3. Repeat the same for the following cells A6 = 16, A7 = 14 and A8 = 23

For the result, move the **Insertion block** to any empty cell of your choice and type the following:

1. =**MIN(A4:A8)** this should give you the smallest number in the range which is 9
2. =**MAX(A4:A8)** this should give you the largest number in the range which in our example, is = 23
3. =**SMALL(A4:A8, 2)** however, this will produce the second smallest number in the range, or 14
4. =**LARGE(A4:A8,3)** on the other hand, this will produce the third largest number in the range, or 16
5. =**AVERAGE(A4:A8)** the system should give you the average of all the numbers entered so far, or 16.40
6. =**SUM(A4:A8)** with this formula, the system should produce the total sum of your numbers.

To view the list of predefined functions currently available in your Microsoft Excel, hold down the **Shift** key and press **F3**. This simple action will take you to a **Paste Function** window—Excel 2000 or **Insert Function** window—Excel 2002. The following is taken from Excel 2002.

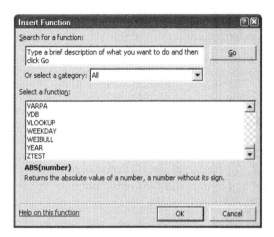

If you are using Excel 2000, under **Function category,** click **All** (in Excel 2002, you will find **All** in the box next to **Or select a category**) and that should lead to a long list of all available **Functions** showing under **Function name.** When you click on any of the functions, you should see explanation of the function showing at the bottom of the window.

Editing in Excel

Ok, you made a mistake in entering text, number or formula, right? To err is human. So my friend, welcome to the human family. You are going to move the **Insertion block** over to the cell to be edited but try not to press any key on the keyboard. As soon as you hit any key, the content of the cell will immediately be replaced. But before I show you how to correct the mistake using your keyboard, let's look at how you can edit using your mouse.

1. Click the **Cell** where the mistake appears and this should display the cell entry in the **Formula bar** ⏷ ✗ ✓ *ƒx*

2. Move the **Mouse pointer** to the Formula bar where the cell entry appears and click, and this should activate the cursor.

3. Use the left ⬅ arrow key on your keyboard or the right ➡ arrow key to move the cursor to where your mistake is and press **Backspace** to erase each character to the left of the cursor, or

4. Press the **Delete** key to erase each character to the right of the cursor, or

5. Use the mouse to select (highlight) characters and type a replacement.

6. When you finish,

a. Click the **Enter** button on the **Formula bar** or press the **Enter** key to accept the changes, or

b. Click the **Cancel** button on the **Formula bar** or press the **Esc** key to abort the changes.

Using the Keyboard to Edit

As stated in the previous section, editing with the mouse can sometimes prove difficult and almost impossible to do without deleting the content of a cell or group of cells. Here is a better and more efficient way to edit the content of a cell or group of cells, even hyperlink without using the mouse.

1. Use the **arrow keys** to select (highlight) the cell you want to edit.

2. Press **F2** to edit the cell contents—this action will immediately place the cursor at the end of the cell entry.

3. Use the **Backspace** to delete to the right or use the left **Arrow key** on your keyboard to move to the exact point where you want to edit.

4. When you have finished, just press **Enter** to accept your changes, or press **Esc** to cancel the changes (in case you change your mind).

AutoSum

One common calculation function in Excel is the **Sum** function. The main focus is simply to manipulate all the numbers in a range of cells either by adding them together or looking for minimum, maximum, average and or weighted average. For example let's reproduce the following and carry out the steps enumerated below:

Sales Person	Invoice
Maria	125
Crystal	253
John	350
Ryan	258
Jose	560
Total	**1546**

1. In **A7** type **Total**
2. Move the **Insertion block** to B7 and click the **AutoSum** Σ button on the **Standard** toolbar
3. When the formula =**Sum(B2:B6)** appears, press the **Enter** key on your keyboard or click on the **Enter** button on the toolbar to accept it. That should produce a total of **1546.**

Moving around in Excel

To move:

1. To cell A1 from anywhere in your worksheet, press **Ctrl** + **Home**
2. To the last row and columns containing data, press **Ctrl** + **End**
3. Within the same row, press **Left** or **Right Arrow** key
4. To a specific cell address or named range using the **Go To** feature, press **Ctrl** + **G** or simply press **F5**
5. Within the same column, press the **Up** or **Down Arrow** key
6. To the beginning of the current row, press **Home**
7. Up or down one screen at a time, press **Page Up** or **Page Down**
8. Left or right one screen, press **Alt** + **Page Up** or **Alt** + **Page Down**

Create Vertical Titles in Excel

Excel provides an easy way to create a vertical heading which runs along the side of a table as oppose to above it. Example of vertical title is hereby highlighted in green:

			Financial Report	
MidMed Quarterly Report		First Qrt	Second Qrt	Third Qurt
	Medication Checks	123,975.00	128,695.00	135,274.00
	Therapy	126,879.00	129,821.00	136,189.00
	Case Management	132,843.00	136,925.00	142,764.00
	Total	**383,697.00**	**395,441.00**	**414,227.00**

To reproduce the above example, follow these steps:

1. Select or highlight the cell where you want to insert vertical heading, otherwise you may have to format each heading one-by-one.

2. Click **Format → Cells,** or simply hold down the **Ctrl** key and press **1** (the number One). That will take you to the following dialog window (Excel 2002)

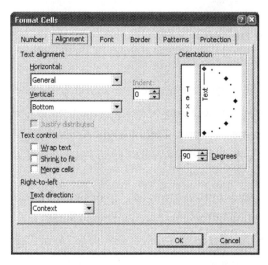

3. Click the **Alignment** tab

4. Increase the **Degrees** text box under *Orientation* to **90.**

5. Select the **Merge cells** text box under *Text Control* and click **OK.**

> If you are unable to produce the expected "Vertical Titles," you may have to create the vertical title of the heading area cell-by-cell. However, the side vertical can be accomplished by simply placing the insertion block one cell below the "Total" and highlight upward. Example: Let's assume the "Total" is in cell A6, you will have to move the insertion block to **A7,** hold down the **Shift** key and press the **Up Arrow** key until A7 through to A1 is selected and then perform the actions stated in Steps 2–5 above.

Saving Files Automatically in Excel 2000

In real life, if you fail to put your valuables away in a safe place, you might end up losing what is so precious and dear to you. To put all burglars and thieves in your surroundings out of business, you need to develop the habit of making sure your stuff are kept in a safe areas before walking away. In Microsoft Excel, it is not unlikely for some unimaginable circumstances to cause you to deviate abruptly from what you are doing, thereby forget to save it. In *Excel 2000*, this type of worry can be dealt with once and for all. *Excel 2000* is fully capable of making sure that all your files are saved before you leave the system. However, the feature that would allow you to enjoy this kind of protection in *Excel 2000* is known as **AutoSave** and it is not installed by default. You will have to install it to use it and here is how:

1. Click **Tools** → and then click **Add-Ins.**
2. Under the **Add-Ins available** list, look for and select the **Autosave Add-in** check box.
3. Click **OK.**

After the Installation, you will have to configure the new feature to use it.

1. Click **Tools** → **AutoSave.**
2. Click to place a check mark next to **Automatic save every.**
3. In the **Minutes** box, enter how often you want Excel to save your workbooks. The default is 10 minutes.
4. If you want the system to let you know before saving, click to place a check mark next to **Prompt Before Saving** box
5. Once you are done, click **OK.**

Moving Between Workbooks or Worksheets in Excel

When you have several workbooks opened with so many worksheets in each workbook, moving around is easier than you think possible. To avoid having to minimize this workbook in other to open that workbook or click on this worksheet and then click on that worksheet, all you have to do is:

1. Press **Ctrl + Tab** to move from one workbook to another workbook,
2. Press **Ctrl + Page Down** to move from one worksheet to another worksheet (from left to right). To move back from worksheet to worksheet (right to left), press **Ctrl + Page Up.**

Enter More Than One Line in an Excel Cell

It is not impossible to enter more than one line of text in a cell or group of cells in Microsoft Excel. In case you need to enter a line break within a cell, follow this step:

1. Hold down the **Alt** key and press the **Enter** key once. This will enable you to start a new line within the same cell.

However, if you should have the need to wrap text automatically to fit the column width, follow these steps:

2. Click the cell of choice to you.
3. Click Format → Cells, and then click the Alignment tab
4. Click the check box next to Wrap text
5. Click Ok.

Data in the cell will wrap to fit the column width. You can make the column wider or narrower to adjust the width of the data.

Excel Shortcuts

Calculate all sheets in all open workbooks	F9
Calculate the active worksheet	SHIFT+F9
Copy	CTRL+C
Create a chart that uses the current range	F11 or ALT+F1
Display the **Format Cells** dialog box	CTRL+1
Display the **Go To** dialog box	F5
Fill the selected cell range with the current entry	CTRL+ENTER
Insert the current time	CTRL+:
Insert today's date	CTRL+;
Move to the beginning of the worksheet	CTRL+HOME
Move to the last cell on the worksheet, which is the cell at the intersection of the rightmost used column and the bottommost used row (in the lower-right corner), or the cell opposite the home cell, which is typically A1	CTRL+END
Open	CTRL+O

Paste	CTRL+V
Paste a function into a formula	SHIFT+F3
Print	CTRL+P
Save	CTRL+S
Select all (when you are not entering or editing a formula)	CTRL+A
Select the current column	CTRL+SPACEBAR
Select the current row	SHIFT+SPACEBAR
Undo	CTRL+Z
When you enter a formula, display the **Formula Palette** after you type a function name	CTRL+A

Exiting Excel

After using Excel or any of the programs/applications in *Microsoft Office* (or any other program for that matter), you should always make the effort to exit the application gracefully. *Microsoft Excel* (like the rest of Office programs) is designed to perform necessary housekeeping before it closes.

If after you click save you decided to modify any of your Excel worksheets and let's assume that changes to the worksheet have not been saved, any attempt to exit will compel Excel to bring out a small pop up window asking the following question:

Do you want to save the changes to "File Name?"

If you want to save all changes, all you need to do is click **Yes** for Excel to save changes to your document before leaving the program, otherwise, click **No**.

When you are inspired by some great purpose, some extraordinary project, all your
thoughts break their bounds: Your mind
transcends limitations, your conscious-
ness expands in every direction, and you
find yourself in a new, great, and wonder-
ful world. Dormant forces, faculties, and
talents become alive, and you discover
yourself to be a greater person by far than
you ever dreamed yourself to be.

—Patanjali

CHAPTER THREE

Managing a Database

To try and explain a program this complex and highly important business tools known as Excel, I am going to employ the use of surgical database aimed at poking into clinical solutions but designed mainly to educate everyone regardless of your professional affiliation. Once you fully understand the entire concept of Excel as revealed in this book, you will be able to apply the knowledge gained to solve any Excel-related problems. Not only that, you will also be able to use the same knowledge when the time comes to cover Visual Basic for Applications (VBA). Chapter Six which deals with Macro provides a way to start digging into VBA and you will find full explanation of its intricacies in my next book.

We are going to attend to some of the requests from Ms. Jones. In case you are wondering who is Ms. Jones, she is our make believe Clinical Director of MidMed—a relatively big Outpatient Psychiatry. First of all, she is asking us to help her Assistant create a Clinical Solution. This is simply a database that can be used to organize patient information and related information such as psychopharmacological treatment (past and present), psychotherapy as well as reimbursement information.

However, the approach I am going to use here slightly deviates from focusing on clinically oriented issues only. It presents a general overview of Excel—one of the most powerful business tools around. The materials covered here are very useful in any professional environment—private or public, for profit or non-profit. For the sake of better understanding, we are going to make some assumptions. We are going to assume that:

1. This clinic (MidMed) does not like randomly generated patient identification number. The Clinical Director would want us to create a unique Patient ID.
2. It is one of the policies of this clinic not to admit any patient less than 5 years old. A patient has to be ? 5 years old.
3. The database must reveal the stated patient age to avoid violation of the policy stated above.

What is a database?

To put simply, a database is a collection of organized records such as library index cards, or phone directory. In a clinical environment, collecting information on patients is without doubt an important process that must be done religiously. We usually start with the basic information such as name, address, phone number and social security number and when we do this per patient, we are in a way creating an individual record.

Excel is all about collecting, analyzing and manipulating data. You can create your own database or use one created by a third party vendor. You might want to create a database to keep track of inventory, clients, customers and patients, or products, employees, including the entity responsible for paying for services rendered.

In creating a database, there are so many things you need to take into consideration. If several people are going to be maintaining the database, you might want to:

1. Consult many of your administrative and clinical staff to be sure no necessary and required item is left out. It is not always easy to modify a large database designed for use in a large business environment.

2. You will need to clearly define particular entries such as "state abbreviation," "date," or special numbers like "social security numbers." This is necessary to eliminate errors.

In this section, you will have the opportunity to:

1. Create a database from the scratch.
2. Prevent invalid data from being entered to eliminate costly error or perhaps conflict with the company's business policy.
3. Add, modify, and delete records in a database using a data form, and
4. Sort your database base on predefined criteria's.

How to create a database

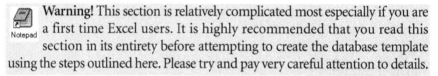 **Warning!** This section is relatively complicated most especially if you are a first time Excel users. It is highly recommended that you read this section in its entirety before attempting to create the database template using the steps outlined here. Please try and pay very careful attention to details.

In this database template example, we are going to create surgical database aimed at poking into clinical solutions. The purpose of it is mainly to educate. In real world, when you create patient admission database, you will have to include Insurance information, Appointments, as well as Patient background history including past treatment history and more. But in this case, many necessary and required fields are going to be intentionally omitted. This is what I meant by "surgical database aimed at poking into clinical solutions." It is a database designed only to explain steps necessary and required to create real database.

Using wizard to create database

Even though we are going to use the Template Wizard to create our first database, it is also possible and perhaps time efficient to accomplish the same goal through direct approach and that is by typing directly into the data grid (Excel worksheet). However, I am going to show you both and which one you prefer is entirely up to you. To create the first database using the *Template Wizard*, do the following:

1. Click **Data → Template Wizard.** If this is your first time of using this feature, it is very likely the command will not appear on the **Data** menu.

a. If you are using *Excel 2000*, click **Tools → Add-Ins** and then select **Template Wizard with Data Tracking,** and click **Ok.** After that, go back to **Data → Template Wizard.**

b. If you are using *Excel 2002 (Excel XP)*, you will have to log on to http://office.microsoft.com and then in the **Search for** box, type **Template Wizard for Excel 2002** and click **Go.** That should take you to a page where you can click on a hyperlink with this heading: Creating a Data Entry Form with the Template Wizard in Excel 2002 or click on Excel 2002 Add-in: Template Wizard with Data Tracking. Feel free to download the **Add-In.** When you have finished downloading, install it right away.

2. Click **Tools → Add-Ins → Template Wizard with Data Tracking → Ok.**

3. Click **Data → Template Wizard** and the following window should pop up

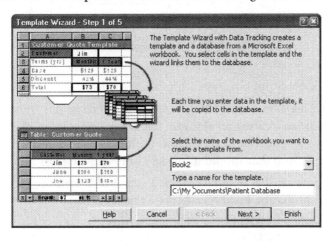

4. In the **Type a name for the template** box, type the following for your data form: *C:\My Documents\Patient Database* and click **Next.** That should take you to the following screen.

5. In the box next to **Select the type of database you want to create** do not change the default **Microsoft Excel Workbook.** Also in the **Type the location and name of the database,** type the following address: *C:\My Documents\Patient Information*

6. Click **Next** and that should lead you to step 3 of 5 of the **Template Wizard** window:

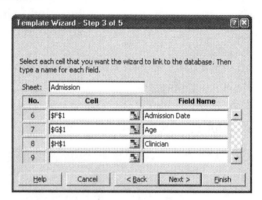

7. In the **Sheet** input box, type *"Admission"* without the quotation marks.

8. In **No. 1 Cell** box, type **$A$1** which is the same as **A1.** By adding the **$** sign, you are creating an absolute cell. More explanation of absolute cell later in the next chapter. To avoid typing, click in cell **A1** on the Excel worksheet and that should input **$A$1** in **No. 1 Cell** box automatically.

9. Click back on the **Template Wizard step 3 of 5** window and in the box directly under the **Field Name** type **Patient ID**

10. Click again in cell **B1** of your Excel worksheet and direct across from **No. 2 Cell** under **Field Name** type **First Name.** Enter the following to complete this step:

	No	Cell	Field Name
a.	No	Cell	Field Name
b.	3	$C$1	Last Name
c.	4	$D$1	SS Number
d.	5	$E$1	D O B
e.	6	$F$1	Admission Date
f.	7	$G$1	Age
g.	8	$H$1	Clinician

11. After entering the last field name, click **Next** to go the next window (step 4 of 5).

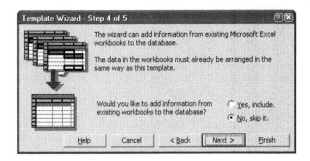

12. From here on, all you need to do is simply click **Next** and that should activate the last window in the **Template Wizard** setup.

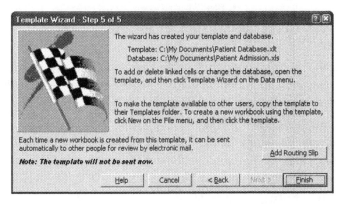

13. Click **Finish** to create your database.

Congratulations, you just created your first database template with the help of the **Template Wizard for Data Tracking.** In some cases your database should appear immediately. But if this does not happen, if your database does not display right away, follow these steps:

1. Click **File → Open**

2. Click the little down arrow next to the **Look in** box and select **Local Disk (C:)**

3. Click **My Documents** directory and when the directory opens, look for an Excel file named; **Patient Information** and click it once to select it.

4. Click **Open** and your Excel worksheet should reveal the following:

	A	B	C	D	E	F	G	H
	Patient ID	First Name	Last Name	SS Number	D O B	Admission Date	Age	Clinician
1								
2								

Adjust Column Width

As you can see, some of your entries are simply too long for the cell in which they appeared. In Microsoft Excel, this is usually no problem. Any text typed in a cell that is too small will just spill over into the next cell only if the next cell is empty. However, if the next cell contains data (any kind of information), then the data in the cell before it will look like part of it is cut off, or truncated, at the cell's border. This can be fixed quickly and easily. To widen a column, follow these steps:

1. Move the **mouse pointer** over to the line between the headers of the column you want to widen. When the mouse pointer reaches the line, it changes from a hollow cross into a double headed solid arrow.

2. Press and **hold down the left mouse** button and drag the border line of the column header to the right until all of its entries appears the way you like, or

3. After step one above, simply **double-click** to size each column automatically to fit its largest entry. This is known as **AutoFit**.

Format Headings

It is a good practice to always distinguish headers from the rest of your worksheet. We did a little bit of this in Volume One of *Beyond Cut, Copy and Paste*. Now let us try it again using the **Format Cells** dialogue window. The steps required to achieve this simple goal are hereby explained:

1. Select or highlight the cell or range of cells you want to format. In our case, move your mouse to **A1**, hold down the **Shift** key on your keyboard and press the **Right Arrow** key on your keyboard until your entire heading from "Patient ID to Clinician" are highlighted.

2. Click **Format → Cells** and then choose the **Font** tab

3. Under **Font**, scroll down and pick **Times New Roman**. Under **Font Style**, click **Bold**, go to **Size**, scroll down and pick **11**, and finally, click the box under **Color** and from the drop down color palette, click **White**

4. Click the **Patterns** tab and from the color palette, pick **Dark Blue**

5. Click **Ok.** When you finished, your database headings should look like the following:

Patient ID	First Name	Last Name	SS Number	D O B	Admission Date	Age	Clinician
JL9999	Judy	Lombardi	021-32-9999	7/24/1988	2/22/2003	15	Mindbender, MD
LF9898	Lori	Forget	023-57-9898	3/21/1990	1/22/2003	14	Langhorne, MD
MB9797	Michael	Bordini	781-77-9797	4/30/1981	3/1/2003	22	Middletown, MD

Define or Restrict column(s) in database

In Microsoft Excel, you have the option to define or restrict a column or columns as needed depending on your corporate policy or a specific need. This is a logical thing to do most especially if you are in an environment where many people are entering data into the same data base at the same time or at different time. Follow these steps to define and restrict some of the columns in the database we are creating for MidMed.

1. Move your mouse to column **A2** click and type this formula: =**Left(B2)&Left(C2)&Right(D2,4)**. I'm quite sure you remember this formula from Volume One of Beyond Cut, Copy and Paste.

2. Click column **E2,** and then click **Data → Validation** and that should lead you to the following **Data Validation** window:

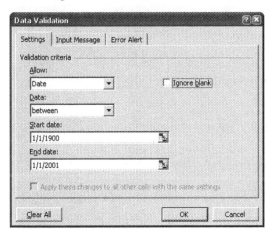

3. Under **Validation criteria,** click the **Allow** box to select **Date**

4. Click in the **Start date** and type this date: **01/01/1900**

5. In the **End date** box, type **01/01/2001**

6. Click the **Input Message** tab.

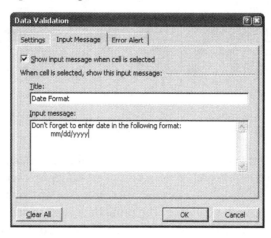

7. Type *"Date Format"* in the **Title** input box, press the **Tab** key to go to the next input box

8. In the **Input message** box, type: *"Don't forget to enter date in the following format: mm/dd/yyyy."* After that,

9. Click the **Error Alert** tab and

10. In the **Title,** type *"You are Unbelievable."*

11. In the **Error message** box, type these words:

    "Are you really going to admit a 3 year old? This is a psychiatric clinic. Let's say that he runs around a lot and plays with too many toys at the same time. Is that not age appropriate? Wait until he is over 5 years old."

12. Click **Ok** to complete this data validation process.

13. Go back to your database and move your mouse over to **G2** and type this formula: =DatedIf(E2,Today(),"Y").

Let us carefully examine what we just did.

- We ask the system to generate **Patient ID** automatically by using what we call concatenation. We asked the system to take the first letter of the first name and add the first letter of the last name plus the last four digit of the social security number.

- In the **D O B** column, we instructed the system not to allow the intake office to admit any child who is not yet 5 years old (this could have been better handled using programming codes).

- Finally, in the **Age** column (the one you are familiar with), it is always good to keep track of the ages of our patients.

> Notepad   Wow! It is amazing that we typed that message in step 10 above. Anyway, that kind of message is not recommended in anyway, shape or form. It was designed to amuse you—that's all. When you are actually dealing with the real thing, try to be friendly.

Anyway, we can now move on to the next level and that is to add information to the database.

Add Records

Even though it is easy to add records, or make changes to a database directly in the worksheet. But when you have a large database, keeping track of what row and which column to modify may be difficult at times. Not only that, it is easy to make mistakes such as inadvertently delete predefined formula or restrictions. It is therefore not a good practice to type directly into your database. Always use the data form to add records

A data form gives you a familiar environment of a typical dialog box to work with. With a data form, it is easy to make changes without running into costly mistakes. You can also use it to locate a record quickly and easily. To add a new record to our database, such as a new patient, etc,

1. Click **any cell** in the second row. This is necessary due to the fact that we currently do not have any record in this database, otherwise, it would not have mattered which row and cell you click.

2. Click **Data → Form** and that should bring up the following input **Admission** window:

First of all, let me explain how we got the **Admission** form. You remember when we created the **Patient Information** database using the **Template Wizard;** we typed the word *"Admission"* in the **Sheet** dialog box. This was done in the **Template Wizard, step 3 of 5.** When we opened the same database in other to add records, the database is showing one worksheet instead of the usual three worksheets Excel is expected to display by default. The only worksheet currently showing in our **Patient Information** database is named **Admission,** hence the **Admission** forms.

As to why the *Patient ID* and the *Age* fields are not accessible on the Admission form, As you would recollect, we predefined these two field in the section entitled **Define or Restrict Column(s) in database,** we typed specific formulas in both the **Patient ID** and **Age** columns to let the system know in what format we prefer to have the patient id as well as what age limit should be in the *"Age"* column. In that wise, neither of the two columns can be accessed directly from the **Admission** form. Not only that, we also define the field representing date of birth (DOB). As stated earlier, this type of column restriction can be handled better through the use of programming codes but for now we are just going to accept the little we are able to accomplish using point and click.

Now let us enter the following patient information into the **Admission** form:

First Name: Judy	First Name: Lakita
Last Name: Lombardi	Last Name: Michael
SS Number: 021-32-9999	SS Number: 032-37-9898
D O B: 07/24/1988	D O B: 03/11/2001
Admission Date: 02/01/2003	Admission Date: 02/24/2003
Clinician: Mindbender, MD	Clinician: LuckyYou, MD

The system should be able to supply input required in **Patient ID** as well as **Age** cells. However, the information entered for "Wendy" in the **D O B** cell would lead to the activation of the following annoying popup window with attitude:

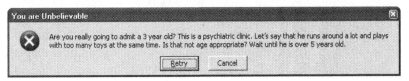

> **You are Unbelievable**
>
> Are you really going to admit a 3 year old? This is a psychiatric clinic. Let's say that he runs around a lot and plays with too many toys at the same time. Is that not age appropriate? Wait until he is over 5 years old.
>
> [Retry]   [Cancel]

The system will only accept one of the two records. It will only accept Judy Lombardi. Wendy is too young to be admitted into this clinic and this is a matter of policy not necessarily a clinically sound decision. If I were you, I would go back and edit that popup message. Anyway, let's add more records by reproducing the following—always use the **Admission** data form:

Patient ID	First Name	Last Name	SS Number	D O B	Admission Date	Age	Clinician
JL9999	Judy	Lombardi	021-32-9999	7/24/1988	2/1/2003	14	Mindbender, MD
LF9898	Lori	Forget	023-57-9898	3/21/1990	1/22/2003	13	Langhorne, MD
MB9797	Michael	Bordini	781-77-9797	4/30/1981	3/1/2003	21	Middletown, MD
JB9696	Jeniffer	Bristol	521-44-9696	12/24/1991	3/11/2003	11	Mindbender, MD
LW9595	Lisa	Walawala	610-21-9595	3/25/1987	2/10/2003	16	Langhorne, MD
LR9494	Lolita	Ringleader	521-45-9494	10/23/1992	2/27/2003	10	Middletown, MD
MC9393	Moisha	Cityview	032-47-9393	11/24/1988	1/27/2003	14	Mindbender, MD
RN9292	Ryan	Norristown	022-35-9292	9/21/1993	2/26/2003	9	Mindbender, MD
KS9191	Kevin	Salem	341-87-9191	7/30/1991	2/23/2003	11	Middletown, MD
LM9090	Lisa	Morrisville	845-21-9090	5/24/1984	3/21/2003	18	Langhorne, MD
JL8888	Jose	Lehigh	408-43-8888	6/24/1990	3/12/2003	12	Mindbender, MD

Modify Records

In case you need to make changes to an existing record in your database, you can easily do it using the data form. Let's assume that the date of birth for Lisa Morrisville was actually 1994 and not 1984 as previous entered, to modify her record, follow these steps:

1. Click any cell within the database
2. Choose **Data → Form** and scroll down to Lisa's record. You can also use **Find Next** to locate Lisa's record.
3. Click in the **D O B** field to change 1984 to 1994
4. After all the changes are made, click **Close**

Sort Data

Sorting data in a large database is highly unavoidable in some business environment. Sorting a database makes it easier to isolate a group of information. In some cases, it may become necessary to sort patient database to isolate every patient belonging to a particular clinician. Let's assume that Dr. Langhorne would like to know his patient case load. Perhaps this is highly important to him due to the fact that he would like to make time for his family or perhaps reduce his case load for health reasons. Whatever the reason, sorting data in Microsoft Excel is as easy as point and click. To sort data (isolate a group of information) follow these simple steps:

Multilevel Sort

1. Click any cell in the database
2. Click **Data → Sort** and that should bring out the following **Sort** Window

3. Under **Sort by,** click to select the first field (or key) for your sort. In this case, let's select **Patient ID** and don't forget to let the system know if you want to sort in **Ascending** or **Descending** order.

4. Select the second field—**Last Name** and then click **Ascending** or **Descending**

5. Select the third field to sort by—**Clinician** and click **Ascending** or **Descending**

Even though the database arrangement has changed by grouping each Clinician case load one after another, but that did not isolate the case load of Dr. Langhorne. Before we address that issue, let us look into a much simpler way we could have performed the sort and that is through a single level sort.

Perform a single level sort

1. Click the field by which you want to sort. In this case, let us click the Clinician field

2. Click the Sort Ascending button ↕ on the Standard toolbar to sort the clinician column in ascending order, or

3. Click the Sort Descending button ↕ on the Standard toolbar to sort the column in descending order.

Filter Data in a Database

To truly isolate the patient caseload of Dr. Langhorne, we are going to employ the use of an Excel feature known as **Filter.** When you ask Excel to *Filter* a database, it responds by displaying only the records that match the criteria you select and the rest of the record will be completely out of view temporarily. In that wise, you can choose to print the displayed records or simply send them into a separate worksheet. To isolate all the patient of Dr. Langhorne using the process of filtering, follow these steps:

1. Click any cell in the database

2. Choose **Data → Filter → AutoFilter**

As you can see, Excel adds an arrow to the right of each field in your database. To complete your database filtering, all you need to do is click the arrow next to the *Clinician* field to activate its drop down list. A list should appear show-ing the following information:

> [All]
> [Top 10…]
> [Custom]
> Langhorne, MD
> Middletown, MD
> Mindbender, MD

Try and click on **Langhorne, MD** and that should isolate and display the cur-rent patient caseload of Dr. Langhorne with the remaining part of the database temporarily out of view. If you are wondering as to the purpose of the first three fields, they are as following:

[All]	Displays all the records for that field, it will take you back to where you were before the filtering option.
[Top 10…]	Displays the top 10 of the clinician record you select from the dialog
[Custom]	Displays records according to the criteria you specify. You might want to use this option to display only patients that are equal to or greater than 10 years old.

Delete Records

You can quickly delete from your database, any record you no longer need. When this is done using the data form, any range such as sum previously defined by the database will be automatically adjusted. To delete a record

1. Click any cell within the database
2. Go to **Data → Form**
3. Scroll to the record you want to delete and click **Delete**
4. Choose **Ok** to confirm the deletion. Do the same (repeat the above steps) to delete additional records as needed.
5. Click **Close**

Add or Delete Worksheets

Each workbook usually gives you three worksheets by default. Depending on your need, you can add more worksheets or delete extra sheets if you like. However, using the Template Wizard to create our database would have forced the system to give you one worksheet, only, to work with.

To add more, follow these steps:
1. Click the existing worksheet tab
2. Choose **Insert** → **Worksheet**

To delete a worksheet

1. Click the tab of the worksheet you would like to remove
2. Choose **Edit** → **Delete Sheet**
3. Click **Ok**

Rename a Worksheet

In case the name you gave a worksheet is not descriptive enough, you have the option to rename. One thing you have to understand is that using a descriptive name will help you and other users to quickly identify the type of data contained on each sheet. Follow these steps to rename a worksheet:
1. Double-click the tab of the worksheet you want to rename
2. Type the new name for the worksheet and you will discover that what you type replaces the existing name
3. Press the **Enter** key

> Another way to **Add, Delete,** or **Rename** a worksheet is to right-click on the sheet tab. A shortcut menu appears. Notepad From the shortcut menu, you can select **Insert** to add new worksheet, or **Delete** to remove any unwanted worksheet, or **Rename** to change the name of the worksheet to something more descriptive.

The truth about the Template Wizard

Needless to say, the template wizard is good and very helpful but could you believe that you seriously do not need it to create a database template! Microsoft intentionally left it out of *Excel 2002* for a reason and placed it on a remote Internet Island. Unless you are led to where it is by one of the citizens of this island (like I did a little while ago), you will never know where it is. But no matter what the reason for Microsoft not including it in *Excel 2002*, it is always good to know how to use it. Let's face it, how would you feel if you are in one of these IT conferences or meetings with your girlfriend or your wife, and this strange looking guy walks up to you, telling you about how he created the best database in the universe with the help of the **Template Wizard**! And the most beautiful woman standing next to you is going really! And you are scratching your head trying to figure out what in the universe is this stranger up to! Now you can let whoever it is know that *Direct Approach* (DA) is better.

What is Direct Approach?

As defined earlier, a database is a collection of records. Each record contains related information about a single item such as an employee. Each record is divided into fields such as the employee's first name, last name, social security number, phone number, address, city, state, zip code, etc. With *Excel 2002*, you can create any database by entering the fields name directly onto your Excel worksheet. This is what **Direct Approach** is all about. It is the fastest way to create a database outside of the **Template Wizard.** To try out **DA,** follow these steps:

1. Open Microsoft Excel
2. Click **A1** and type your database field names directly (as specified earlier) onto worksheet1 beginning at column **A1** and use the tab key to move from column **A1** to **B1** and so on and so forth.
3. Adjust and format each column as necessary
   a. Select the field names and click **Format → Cell**
   b. Click the **Font** tab and under **Font Style,** select **Bold,** under **Size,** select 11 and under color, select **White.**
   c. Click **Patterns** tab and select **Dark Green**
   d. Click **Ok**
4. Enter necessary formulas to define the appropriate fields such as **Patient ID** and **Age.**

5. Move the insertion block to the column under the **D O B** field and click **Data → Validation** and follow the previous steps outlined earlier for **Data Validation**

6. Click **Data → Form** to populate your database.

About the guy at the IT conference; now you can say to him: hey pal! you could have avoided using such a long and time consuming process, and just type your database field directly into your worksheet, save it as a template and when the time comes, use the data **Form** to populate your database. Guess who would be going, really! One more thing, tell him to go and get a copy of this book *"Unlock Microsoft Excel."*

> You cannot achieve a new goal by applying the same level of thinking that got you where you are today.
> —Albert Einstein

CHAPTER FOUR

Formulas and Functions

One of the most amazing features of Excel is its ability to help people solve number problems. With formulas, you can perform any calculation based on a data set. The type of calculations you can perform ranges from just a simple calculation such as adding a block of numbers to dealing with complex calculation such as trying to determine monthly payment on a $125,000 mortgage loan amortized over 30 year period at 5.75% interest rate.

In chapter one, you learned how to perform those simple calculations and here we are going to take it a step further by showing you how to create and perform complex formulas.

On the other hand, a function is a preprogrammed calculation. All you need to do is recall the function and provide it with some information using the proper syntax and when this is done, it is certain the system would give you the expected answer. For example, let us try to calculate monthly payment on the mortgage scenario created in paragraph one above.

Description	Data
Annual Interest Rate	5.75%
Number of months of payments	360
Amount of Loan	$125,000.00
Monthly Payment	$729.47

In this scenario, I am going to use a function known as **PMT** for payment function, and instruct the system to perform calculations using the correct order of operations =PMT(B2/12,B3,B4. Now, let us look carefully at the formula in the light of the only function employed.

1. I recalled the PMT function (don't forget, every formula must begin with the equal (=) sign.

2. I then instructed the system to take the annual interest rate and divide it by the number of months per year.

3. The next step is to simply follow the format required by Excel 2002. The total number of payments is actually taken from the number of months per year multiply by the number of years representing the duration of the loan which is 12*30 = 360.

4. The last item on the formula based on the function is to supply the loan amount which is $125,000.

5. If the monthly payment shows a negative number instead of positive, simply add negative sign (minus sign) after the equal (=) sign but before the **PMT** function and the result would come out as positive number. When you finish typing the formula, it should look like the following: =-PMT(B2/12,B3,B4)

How to Calculate Amortization

	A	B	C	D	E
1	Number of Years	30			
2	Interest Rate	5.87%			
3	Principal	125000			
4	Payment	=-PMT(b2/12,b1*12,b3)			
5					
6	Balance	Interest	Principal Paid	Pre-Paid	New Balance
7	=b3	=a7*b2/12	=b4-b7	100	=a7-c7-d7
8	=e7	=a8*b2/12	=b4-b8	100	=a8-c8-d8
9	=e8	=a9*b2/12	=b4-b9	100	=a9-c9-d9

How to evaluate formulas one expression at a time

A formula may appears to be entered correctly but the order of the functions or operations may not be correct. To be sure you will always get the expected result, Microsoft includes a friendly feature that will allow you to evaluate formulas and this feature is known as (guess what!) **Evaluate Formula**. When it comes to assessing every part of a formula, most especially nested formulas, there is no better tool. Evaluate Formula is designed to help you zero in on the specific part of a formula that may not be working the way you expect.

Every programmer is familiar with debugging tool available in programming environment; Evaluate Formula works the same in Excel environment. Let's say we have a database that look like the following:

Period	First Quarter Cash Flow Need	
	Cash on hand	Account Receivable
January	8848	35478
February	7984	27934
March	2932	42581
Evaluation	105993	

We enter the following formula in cell B7:

$$=IF(AVERAGE(B3:B5)<55000,SUM(C3:C5),0)$$

The result revealed the total of our Account Receivable because Cash on hand is less than $55,000. Let us look carefully at the structure of our formula and you will discover that what we are trying to do is determine if we are going to see the bank manager for a line of credit or go for receivable factoring in the light of our strong Account Receivable (AR). The formula says: if the average of the values in cells B3 through B5 is less than $55,000 then evaluate and give us the sum of the values in cells C3 through C5, otherwise, return 0. In other word, we would like to know—if the average of our cash on hand for the first quarter is less than $55,000 If that is the case, the second part of our formula is asking the system to tell us the current face value of our account receivable. To use the *Evaluate Formula* feature in Excel, follow these steps:

1. Click **Tools → Formula Auditing → Evaluate Formula** and that should lead you to the following dialog window

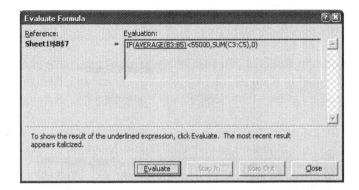

2. To show the result of the underlined expression, click **Evaluate** and that should produce the result of the first part of the formula as following

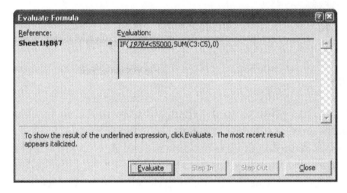

3. The first part of the expression reveals an average value of $19,764 which is less than $55,000

4. Click **Evaluate** again to see the result of the second part. This second part simply evaluates to true or false in the light of the overall value of our account receivable which in this case is $105,993.

If you are using Excel 2002 otherwise known as Excel XP, there is another option called **Show Calculation Steps**. This is available on the **Error Checking Options** smart tag menu. Basically, this option operates in a way similar to Evaluate Formula. However the only difference is that the first expression is already evaluated when the dialog box is displayed.

Let us take it one step further by changing the value of our Cash Flow for each month, thereby producing an average greater than $55,000. What do you think would be the result in response to our formula? What this means is that there is no need, right now, to borrow or rush out in favor of receivable factoring. The panic level is equal to **Zero** because the average of our cash flow for the three periods revealed is greater than **$55,000** and the same with AR. In this case, we are doing fine.

First Quarter Cash Flow Need		
Period	Cash on hand	Account Receivable
January	51879	35478
February	56545	27934
March	62954	42581
Evaluation	0	

Name Box

At the top of Excel gridline, to the right of the formula bar is where you will find the name box. Name box displays the address of the active cell. If your insertion block is in **A1**, the name box will read A1. To put simply, the main purpose of the name box is to display the address of the active cell but you can use the Name box to name a cell or group of cells. Instead of A1, B2, C34, D23, and so on and so forth, you can give each cell a more descriptive name. When a cell is given a name, you can refer to it from anywhere within your worksheet without having to worry about its cell number. It provides a more efficient way to handle cell referencing within formulas and functions. For example, let us take a careful look at the following calculations:

Income	Monthly Total
Full Time	$3,875.00
Part Time	962.00
Consulting Services	1,174.00
Total Income	**6,011.00**

1. Click cell **B2** and the Name box should read B2
2. To replace the B2 with a more descriptive name, click in the **Name** box and the B2 showing should be highlighted right away
3. Type **Full_Time** to replace the B2 name
4. Click cell **B3** and in the Name box, type **Part_Time.**
5. Click cell **B4** and also in the Name box, type **Consulting** and finally
6. Click cell **B5** and type **Total_Income** in the Name box.

Please note that in typing those names, I typed underscore instead of space. The use of space would have resulted in syntax error. This shall be explained in full when we get to programming in Visual Basic for Applications (VBA).

> Even though I did not specifically ask you to type the labels in column A, it is highly recommended that you include both the headings and all the information in column A. The information you input into column "A" are strictly *Labels* and the one typed into the Name box for column B represent *Cell Reference.*

Now that we have changed the cell name reference, let us enter the formula for Total Income as following: =Full_Time+Part_Time+Consulting

Cell References in Formulas

Here, I am going to discuss three different kinds of cell references. They are: Relative, Absolute, and Mixed cell references. Anything about statistics and the discussion of the steps leading to the conclusion of statistical analysis are relatively boring to most people but highly essential in life and when the time comes, most people usually wish they had paid attention to all its nitty-gritty.

Absolute Reference

Most of the formulas I have used up to this point had been **Relative Reference** formulas. For example, suppose you have a worksheet like the following:

	A	B	C
1		January	February
2	Brooklyn Clinic	67954	72836
3	Princeton Clinic	58721	63147
4	Philadelphia Clinic	64121	68932
5	Total	=Sum(B2:B4)	

When you copy the formula in cell B5 to cell C5, you will discover that the references has changed to =Sum(C2:C4) and the same thing would happen when you copy further to cell D5. It will immediately assume appropriate cell references and the formula would look like this =Sum(D2:D4). This is due to the fact that a relative cell points *only* to a cell position *relative* to the formula's location. To put simply, each time you copy a formula with relative cell references, the formula along with its references will adjust automatically to reflect its new position.

Absolute Reference

There are times when you would not want the references to be adjusted automatically to avoid getting an incorrect answer or in some cases, an error message. For example, let us take another look at the same worksheet:

	A	B	C	D
1		January	February	Percentage of January Sales
2	Brooklyn Clinic	67954	72836	=B2/$B$5
3	Princeton Clinic	58721	63147	
4	Philadelphia Clinic	64121	68932	
5	Total	=Sum(B2:B4)		

Please bear in mind that an **Absolute cell reference** clearly defines the cell you would not want adjusted when you copy the formula. To create absolute cell reference, the rule of thumb is to type a $ (dollar sign) in front of both the column letter and row number of the cell you want to see remain constant. The formula in the worksheet above reads: =B2/$B$5 as oppose to =B2/B5. There is no doubt that =B2/B5 would have given us the correct answer in column D2 only. But when the same formula is copied to cell D3, it will adjust automatically to:

=B3/B6, thereby result in an incorrect answer or error message if column B6 is an empty column. To avoid this kind of incorrect answer or error message, we employed the use of absolute cell reference.

An absolute cell reference simply does not adjust when the original formula is copied to a new column. In this case, the formula =B2/$B$5 would produce correct answer in D2 and when the same formula is copied to cell D3, the new formula would read; =B3/$B$5 and also produce a correct answer. The only absolute part of this formula is the divisor and the divisor in our example is the *Total* sale for the month of January.

Mixed Cell References

On the other hand, there are instances whereby you would not want to keep an entire column absolute. In that case, all you need to do is employ the use of **mixed cell reference.** A mixed cell reference is a reference in which only part of the cell—perhaps the column letter or row number is absolute as in $B5 or B$5. For example let us recall the same worksheet to calculate percentage of February sales. We are going to change the formula in D2 to =B2/B$5 as in the following:

	A	B	C	D	E
1		January	February	Percentage of January Sales	Percentage of February Sales
2	Brooklyn Clinic	67954	72836	=B2/B$5	
3	Princeton Clinic	58721	63147		
4	Philadelphia Clinic	64121	68932		
5	Total	=Sum(B2:B4)	=Sum(C2:C4)		

As you are well aware by now, when the formula in cell D2 is copied to cell D3, it changes to =B3/B$5. Let us look carefully at the anatomy of our formula. In the first cell reference, the row number is relative, in that wise, it is adjusted by one due to the fact that the formula was copied one row down. However, the second cell reference (B$5), is not adjusted because it is absolute. But when the same formula is copied across to cell E2, the formula will change to =C2/C$5. One interesting thing here is how the column letter has changed in both cell references because it is relative.

Number Formats

Each time you enter a number into an unformatted cell, Excel displays the number exactly as entered. If you enter 52978.00 Excel will display the number and drop the trailing zeros after the decimal point. Not only that, if your number is larger than the cell, it is highly likely Excel will change it into scientific notation format. If you are an Accountant, you would want your negative number to display to reflect the actual result of your computation. For example, some individuals are especially concerned about how negative numbers are displayed—some would prefer to see negative numbers display in red while others would prefer to use parenthesis or perhaps simply show a minus sign before the numbers. Regardless of your preferences, Excel makes it easier for you to format numbers in a variety of ways. Number formats can only change the way numbers are displayed but not the actual numbers. To format numbers, do the following:

1. Highlight all the cells containing the numbers you want to format.

2. Click **Format → Cells...**and that should take you to the following window:

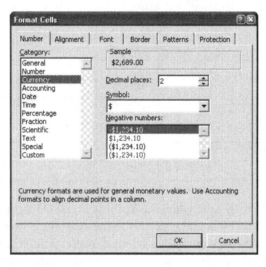

3. Click the **Number** tab (if not already activated) and you will see all the choices under **Category**. There you will find choices that allow you to apply the currency, comma, or percentage number style.

IF Function and the Lookup Functions

Depending on the structure of your worksheets, there are some functions designed to help you make decisions based upon the values entered in another cell. One of those functions is the **IF** function. The result returned by the **IF** function is dependent upon whether a logical condition is true or false. Other functions include **HLOOKUP** and **VLOOKUP**. Both of these functions return values from lookup tables.

IF Function

If you are a payroll specialist who is concerned about payroll deductions, making sure that they are calculated properly and appropriately, and that each employee's paycheck reflects their true compensation, you will find these functions helpful. If you are an accounting manager endowed with the task of making sure the correct commission is paid at the right time to your sales force, you will find these functions helpful. The IF function uses a logical operator such as > (**greater than**) or < (**less than**) to evaluate a condition. Any of the following logical operators can be used with the IF function:

Logical Operator	Description
=	Equal
<	Less Than
>	Greater Than
>=	Greater than or equal to
<=	Less than or equal to
<>	Not equal to

The general syntax of the IF function is =**IF(Comparison,True,False)**. In a real world, it would be difficult to find employee who will work for commission if the rule is too strict and highly inflexible. For example, if you are trying to motivate your sales team to sell $10,000 and make 20% commission (very generous pay by the way) but offers no commission when individual sale is less than $10,000, you may find yourself doing all the work alone and your time is fractured between having to do administrative work as well as attending to customers. On the other hand, if you create an environment whereby members of your sales team are compensated using graduated commission table, you would not only sell a lot, somehow, you would discover that you have one of the best sales team in the industry. The following is an example of a graduated commission table paying 20% commission if sales is >= 10,000. To produce expected result, enter the following into your Excel worksheet:

	A	B	C	D	E
1	Monthly Commission Calculations				
2	February 2003 Report				
3					
4	Medical Equipment	February	Com. Rate	Total Com.	Evaluation
5	Bob Doe	12000			
6	Rick Maldonado	8957			
7	Tanisha Brown	14721			
8	Michael Douglas	9897			

1. Enter the information presented in column **A1, A2**, and skip **A3**
2. Complete the headings in Row 4. Enter Medical Equipment in **A4**, February in **B4**, Com. Rate in **C4**, Total Com in **D4** and Evaluation in **E4**
3. Enter employee's names in column **A** beginning at **A5**
4. Enter sales figures in column **B** directly across from each name
5. In column **C5**, enter this formula =IF(B5>=10000,20%,10%) and use the fill handle to copy the formula to **C6, C7** and **C8**
6. Enter this formula =B5*C5 in column **D5** and use the fill handle to copy the formula to **D6, D7** and **D8**. When you finish, your Excel worksheet should look like the following:

Monthly Commission Calculations				
February 2003 Report				
Medical Equipment	February	Commission Rate	Total Commission	Evaluation
Bob Doe	12,000.00	20%	2,400.00	
Rick Maldonado	8,957.00	10%	895.70	
Tanisha Brown	14,721.00	20%	2,944.20	
Michael Douglas	9,897.00	10%	989.70	

Vlookup Function

The **VLOOKUP** otherwise known as the Vertical Lookup and the **HLOOKUP** also known as the Horizontal Lookup functions are designed to look up values in tables such as tax tables, commission rate tables and any other tables. The syntax for the **VLOOKUP** which is used more often is =**VLOOKUP(search argument, lookup table, column number)** Let us take a careful look at the VLOOKUP function and its components in the following worksheet:

	A	B	C	D
1	Sales	February Sales	Commission Rate	Evaluation
2	Ryan Michael	12,500		
3				
4				
5	Sales Volume	Commission Rate	Evaluation	
6	-	0%	Under Achiever	
7	8,000	10%	Below Quota	
8	10,000	15%	Below Quota	
9	15,000	20%	Above Quota	
10	20,000	22%	Above Quota	
11	25,000	25%	Over Achiever	

There are two major parts to this worksheet—the outcome part which you will find between **A1** and **D2** and the lookup table located between **A5** and **C11**. The lookup table is more like a storage area and can be located anywhere (possibly out of sight) within the same worksheet as the outcome portion. By the same token, you can also keep the lookup table on a separate worksheet.

The use of Watch Window

The **Watch Window** provides a way for you to see what is going on in another cell without having to scroll to the actual cell. For example, let's say you are entering data in cell **A89** which is likely to affect the result of a formula you entered in cell C12. Instead of scrolling back to cell C12 to see the result of the formula, you can actually see the value of the formula change from within the watch window even if you are currently entering data in cell A89.

Not only that, with the help of the *Watch Window*, you can even watch values on other sheets or in other workbooks. To activate the **Watch Window**, follow these steps:

1. Right-click the cell where you are currently entering data
2. Click **Add Watch** and that would immediately activate the **Watch Window**
3. On the **Watch Window**, click **Add Watch** and that should lead you to the following popup dialog box:

4. Type the cell address where you entered the formula and
5. Click **Add** and that should lead to a result similar to the following

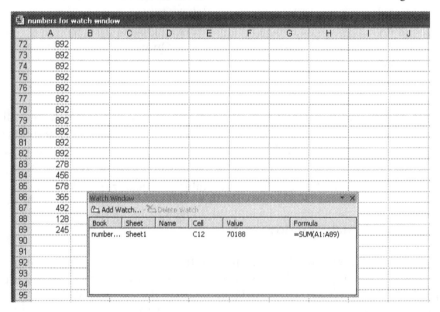

Generate Random Numbers.

When the contents of an Excel spreadsheet are not given, you can use randomly generated numbers to quickly populate the spreadsheet. There is a function specially designed to make generating numbers randomly easy to accomplish. This function is known as RAND function. To use it, follow these steps:

1. Click any cell to produce a number between 0 and 1 and type =**RAND()**, or

2. Click any cell (usually cell **A1** if this is a blank worksheet) to generate a number between 1 and 100, type =**RAND()*100**.

3. To populate a spreadsheet, use the fill handle as following to quickly populate as many cells as you'd like with random numbers:

   a. Click the cell where the first number appears

   b. Move your mouse to the bottom right corner of the insertion □⬚ block—right on top of the little dark square block and your cursor will then turn into a little plus sign.

   c. While your mouse is on the tinny dark square block, click and hold down the left mouse button and drag across to cover as many cells as you want

   d. Repeat step **3b** and **3c** above but drag down the mouse to cover as many cells and release the mouse when you are done.

> ⬚ To change the number format of your random numbers (for
> Notepad example, if you'd prefer whole numbers to decimal points),
> click **Cells** on the **Format** menu. In the Format Cells dialog box,
> click the **Number** tab and then click **Number** in the **Category** list.
> Then in the **Decimal places** box, enter the number zero and click **Ok.**

Tools to perform a statistical analysis

I just want to bring to your attention the fact that you can use Microsoft Excel to assist you in your quest for accurate statistical analysis. My intent is not to teach statistical analysis but to let you know that these tools are available should you need to use them. Most of what you will need is available in one of Excel features known as **Data Analysis**. It is highly likely that *Data Analysis* may not be available to use right away. This does not mean you bought the wrong version of Microsoft Excel. It simply means that you will have to add *Data Analysis* to your system. To install and use *Data Analysis* Add in, follow these steps:

1) On the **Tools** menu, click **Data Analysis**. If **Data Analysis** is not available, you will need to load the *Analysis ToolPak*. To do that, follow the steps below:

   (i) On the **Tools** menu, click **Add-Ins.**

   (ii) In the **Add-Ins available** list, select the **Analysis ToolPak** box, and then click **OK.** Go back to step One.

2) When you see the following **Data Analysis** dialog box pops up,

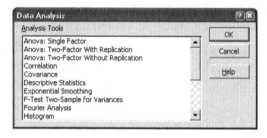

3) Click the name of the analysis tool you want to use, and then click **OK**.

4) Each analysis tool would lead you to a dialog box for the tool you selected in order to set the analysis options you want.

The following example is taken from an actual record of some outpatient medical clinics and the data are recorded in million. It is hereby presented with the intent to explain how best to handle calculating standard deviation in Excel spreadsheet. Lower standard deviation is usually regarded as an indicator of stability while higher standard deviation is regarded as higher volatility.

	A	B	C
1	Year	Average Yearly Visit	Squared Deviation
2	1994	4.9	0.96
3	1995	5.4	0.23
4	1996	5.9	0.00
5	1997	5.1	0.60
6	1998	5.6	0.08
7	1999	5.8	0.01
8	2000	6.9	1.04
9	2001	6.4	0.27
10	2002	6.9	1.04
11		Total of Column "C"	4.24

The formula for the Squared Deviation typed in cell C2 is: =(B2-AVERAGE (B$2:B$10))^2 and to get the Standard Deviation, type either of the following formulas in cell C11:

=STDEVA(B$2:B$10) or =SQRT(C11/(COUNT(B2:B10)-1))

Step by step calculation is as following:

1. You first of all calculate Average of the data set =**AVERAGE(B$2:B$10)**

2. Subtract the average from each year data to find deviation =**B2-AVERAGE (B$2:B$10)**

3. You use the exponential operator which in this case is the ^ (**caret**) sign to obtain the square root of step 2 above =**(B2-AVERAGE (B$2:B$10))^2**

4. Try and obtain the total of the squared deviation using this formula =**SUM(B2:B10)**

5. The formula to obtain the total count of the data set is =**COUNT (B2:B9)-1** and this represent **N-1**

6. We need to divide the squared deviation by the formula in step 5 above. To get that, we have to use this formula =**C11/(COUNT(B2:B10)-1)**

7. Finally, you get the standard deviation using the following formula:
   =**SQRT(C11/(COUNT(B2:B10)-1))**

8. However, if you are using Excel 2000 or Excel XP (2002), the following is all you need:
   =**STDEVA(B$2:B$10)**

Needless to say, this is just one aspect of statistical analysis and the explanations presented here are

Notepad

somehow insufficient for something this complex unless you are well informed in statistical analysis. Should you like to know more about the subject of Statistical Analysis, feel free to visit www.mednetservices.com from time to time for lots of Free downloads.

CHAPTER FIVE

Graphics and Charts

The focus of a Database is to produce expected result. However, there are times when you might want to dress up the worksheet on which all the nitty-gritty of the database resides. Even though looking good is the last thing on the mind of your database development team, however, a well designed database with appropriate graphic or picture can lead to a whole new attitude, perhaps makes it easier to figure out what the database is all about, thereby eliminate barriers to communication.

A policeman stops a lady and asks for her license.
He says "Lady, it says here that you should be wearing glasses."
The woman answered "Well, I have contacts."
The policeman replied "I don't care who you know! You're getting a ticket!"

—Author unknown

For clarity, *Microsoft Excel* makes it possible to insert clip arts, pictures and even company logo in your worksheet. The program comes with so many useful clip arts and if you cannot find appropriate clip art for your project, you have the option to search online (from within the program) for more clip arts. You can also use your own custom designed graphic; company logo, scanned picture or drawings or any work of art generated digitally or otherwise.

If you have used the clip art gallery in *Microsoft Word,* you are probably familiar with how you can insert from the gallery. Even if you are not too familiar, the process is easy to follow.

Insert Clip Arts and Pictures

1. Increase the width of the column (cell) where you want to insert the clip art or increase the width of every column (if you have to) by doing the following:
   a. To increase the width of every column, click the **Select All** button, the block at the top left corner of the gridline—the empty block between the row number 1 and column letter A.
   b. To increase the width of only one column, click the column, and then
   c. Click **Format → Column → Width** to set the width (in this case, let us set it to 18)
2. Change the font to *Times New Roman* and the font size to 11 (this is optional)
3. Click any of the cells to deselect the entire worksheet.
4. Click the **Insert Clip Art** button ▨ on the **Drawing** toolbar usually located at the bottom of your screen (if activated) ╲ ╲ □ ○ 🖾 🖾 ◀ ✿ 🖾 🖾 ◇ ･ ⊿ ･ △ ･ ≡ ☰ 🗐 ■ ▨ or simply
5. Click **Insert → Picture → Clip Art**—either way would lead you to the following screen:

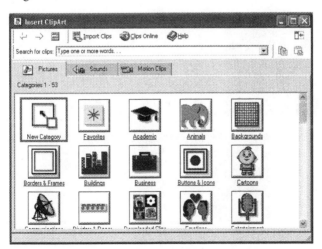

6. Click the **Buildings** category to display clip arts related to buildings most especially if your database is designed to produce amortization or related information

7. Click **any picture** of your choice

8. Move your mouse over the pop-up menu to see the ScreenTip of each button on the pop-up menu.

9. Click the **Preview clip** option on the popup menu to display an enlarged copy of the clip.

10. Click the **Close** button on the **Preview** window. If this is what you are looking for,

11. Click **Insert** on the pop-up menu to insert the picture in your worksheet.

If the clip art you are looking for is not available among those provided with Microsoft Office, you can always go online to find the appropriate one.

12. Click the **Clips Online** button (before you do that, make sure your computer system is already logged on to the Internet). And that should bring out a dialogue window designed to remind you. Do not forget that connecting to the Internet is necessary and required.

13. Click **Ok** if you are connected.

14. To add your custom designed clip arts, company logo, drawing, etc. Click the **Import Clips** to search your system for your company logo, drawing or your unique one-of-a-kind graphic file. Try to reproduce the following example:

RFS, Enterprises
Race For Strength

	Income	Expenses	Net Income
Medicare	$21,875	$12,998	$8,877
Medicaid	$19,894	$11,947	$7,947
HMO	$23,689	$12,947	$10,742
Staffing	$32,169	$11,547	$20,622
	$97,627	$49,439	$48,188

Using the Chart Wizard

There are times when you need to establish comparisons, trends and other relationships. In a way, there are times when you need to help the numbers in a worksheet tell their own story in living color. One of the best ways to convey this is through effective use of charts. A chart can help anyone including those who despise numbers understand the true meaning and relationship between the worksheet data and performance/productivity.

One of the main purposes of a chart is to represent data graphically. Excel makes it possible to create column charts, bar charts, line charts, area charts and pie charts using the Chart Wizard. It also provides a way to edit and format every chart object.

We are going to create a chart with the help of the Chart Wizard from the following worksheet:

	January Sales
Medicare	257895.00
Medicaid	124956.00
HMO	232741.00
Blue Cross	89654.00
C. Ins.	131542.00
Private Pay	46738.00

Create a chart

1. Select the data you want to present graphically as well as the column heading and row label (it is always a good practice to select your data as oppose to defining it during the running of the wizard).

2. Choose **Insert → Chart** or simply click the **Chart Wizard** button on the Toolbar. Either way, you would be led to the following screen from Excel 2000:

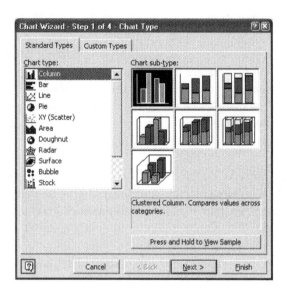

3. Select a chart type from those listed under **Chart Type** and also select a chart sub-type from those listed under **Chart sub-type** (for our sample database, let us pick **Pie** chart).

4. Click **Next** to go to step 2 of 4 of the Chart Wizard. From the step 2 of the Chart Wizard, you will be given the options to choose:

   a. A different range of cells (this is where you define the range if you had not selected your range prior to going into the Chart Wizard).

   b. How to present the chart—Rows or Columns

5. Click **Next** to go to step 3 of 4. Here you will have the option to enter the **Title,** hide the labels on the category axes when you click the **Axes** tab. Click **Gridlines** tab to decide whether your chart should gridlines for the value axes displayed. Click the **Legend** tab to identify the columns. The **Data Labels** tab displays the values from the worksheet on top of the columns. And on the **Data Table,** click the **Show data table** check box and a table will appear below the Preview chart.

6. Click **Next** to go to step 4 (the last step) of the **Chart Wizard** and when the step 4 dialogue window appears, you will be giving two choices.

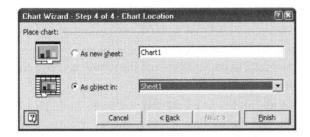

7. Click **As new sheet** to create the chart on a separate sheet, or

8. Click **As object in** to embed the chart in the current worksheet

9. Click **Finish** and your worksheet should look similar to the following:

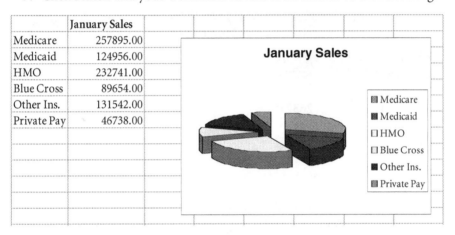

	January Sales
Medicare	257895.00
Medicaid	124956.00
HMO	232741.00
Blue Cross	89654.00
Other Ins.	131542.00
Private Pay	46738.00

Working with Styles

When we talk about *style* in Excel, we are simply talking about cell formatting. A predefined cell formatting can be applied to any cell. Using styles provides some great advantages in comparison to manual formatting.

1. It provides consistency. Once applied, you no longer need to remember what format settings used for specific types of cells.

2. Styles are more convenient. Using styles makes it possible to create reusable format, thereby avoid the monotony of having to repeat the same formatting commands over and again in various cell.

Microsoft Excel makes it possible to create styles from the following two methods:

1. One method is to create style by example. In this case, you manually pick all of the formatting command for a particular cell and then assign style name to the formatting.

2. The second method is to create style by definition. This method allows you to open the dialog box, choose format settings you would like to assign to the style.

To create Styles by Example:

1. Open the *Admission* database created in chapter two

	RFTC Enterprises Mortgage Inc.				
Period	Income				
1st Quarter	23549				
2nd Quarter	26321				
3rd Quarter	27892				
4th Quarter	31875				

2. To add the *Style* button to the Formatting toolbar, right-click on any toolbar and choose **Customize** and then do the following:

   a. Click the **Commands** tab to activate it

   b. Click **Format** under *Categories*

   c. Drag the **Style** box on to the *Formatting* toolbar and release the mouse.

3. Close the *Customize* dialog box. That is all you need to define a Style by Example. For more information visit: www.mednetservices.com

We must use time creatively and forever realize that the time is always right to do great things.

—Martin L. King, Jr.

Chapter Six

Working with Macros and Toolbars

Some of you who bought volume one of *Beyond Cut, Copy and Paste* would remember my extensive coverage of Recording and Playing Macros. This is one of many features that are common to all of *Microsoft Office* programs. Needless to say, there are some tasks that are just too long and at times too technical to repeat over and again. In a busy environment, such a lengthy and highly involved task may often-times result in human error unless something is done to reduce the possibility of unnecessary mistakes.

Macro provides a means to create mini-automation without getting into all the nitty-gritty of programming. A macro provides a way to record a set of steps along with its instructions that can be played back at a later time. Excel's macro is capable of recording keystrokes and any associated command necessary to perform a task.

As you know, creating a database involves a lot of steps. Adding more information to the database shouldn't require so many steps.

1. Open the **Admission** database developed in Chapter Two

2. Choose **Tools** → **Macro** → **Record New Macro**. In the **Macro Name** text box, type a descriptive name in the Macro Name box. Space is an invalid character. Try not to use space in macro names. Let us name the macro *AdmissionMacro*.

3. To assign this macro to a shortcut key, in the Shortcut Key box, type **Q** (this could be any letter of interest to you). The **Ctrl** + would change to **Ctrl** + **Shift** + **?**. This is slightly different from the way Microsoft Word handles assigning shortcut key to macros in Word.

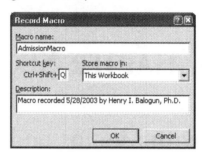

4. In the **Store macro in** box, click to select the location where you want to store the macro. This macro is applicable to the current workbook only. So, we are going to select **This Workbook** option.

5. Click **Ok** to begin recording.

6. Choose **Data** → **Form**

7. When the data **Form** appears, click **Ok**

8. To stop recording, look for the following hanging toolbar:

9. Click on the **Stop Recording** button (the square blue block) on the toolbar. The macro is now ready to be played back.

Running Macro

Once you have recorded a macro, running it is easy. When we were recording the *AdmissionMacro* macro, we assigned the macro to a shortcut **Ctrl** + **Shift** + **Q**. Not only that, we also indicated in the **Store macro in** box that the macro was for **This Workbook**. To run it, make sure that the *Admission* database is open and active on your screen, otherwise it would not work.

Hold down the **Ctrl** + **Shift** key and press **Q**. The data **Form** screen should pop up.

To run a macro from the **T**ools menu, follow these steps:

1. Open the document in which you want to run the macro—in this case, open the *Admission* database.

2. Choose **T**ools → **M**acro → **M**acros.

3. In the list box, select the macro you want to run; (*AdmissionMacro*) then click **Run** to run the macro.

Assigning a Macro to a Button

Once you have created a macro to automate repetitive tasks, you can assign the macro to a toolbar button to make it much easier to use. This way, you don't have to remember a shortcut key combination to use it. This is extremely time effective when your macro is saved to the ***Personal Macro Workbook*** as oppose to ***This Workbook*** option. The only macros available for use in all workbooks are the macros saved to *Personal Macro Workbook*. In that wise, before you assign a macro to a toolbar button, check to see where it is saved. Otherwise, you will end up with a toolbar button that does nothing most of the time.

To assign a macro to a toolbar button, follow these steps:

1. Display the toolbar on which you want to place your macro button (this could be any toolbar—Standard or Formatting).

2. Click **Tools** → **Customize**

3. Click the **Commands** tab

4. Choose **Macros** from the **Categories** list.

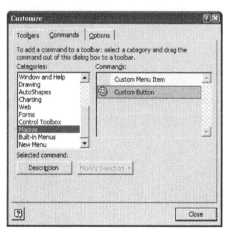

5. Select **Custom Button** under *Commands* list and drag it onto the Standard toolbar. (Remember, you have to drag the *Custom Button* to the toolbar of your choice to activate the *Modify Selection* option.)

6. Click **Modify Selection** and that should activate the following dialogue window:

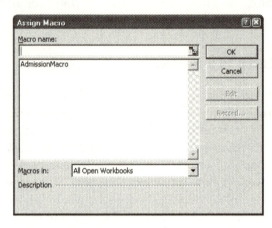

7. Click the macro name **AdmissionMacro** and click **Ok.**

It is the constant and determined effort that breaks down all resistance, sweeps away all obstacles.

—Claude M. Bristol

CHAPTER SEVEN

Producing Worksheet Output

A mother and baby camel are talking one day when the baby camel asks, "Mom why have I got these huge three-toed feet?"

The mother replies, 'Well son, when we trek across the desert, your toes will help you to stay on top of the soft sand."

"Ok" says the son. A few minutes later, the son asks: "Mom, why have I got these great long eyelashes?"

They are there to keep the sand out of your eyes on the trips through the desert," the camel mother answered.

Thanks, Mom," replies the son. After a short while, the son returns and asks, "Mom, why have I got these great big humps on my back?"

The mother, now a little impatient with the baby camel, replies, "They are there to help us store water for our long treks across the desert so we can go without drinking for a long period of time."

"That's great, Mom. So we have huge feet to stop us from sinking, and long eyelashes to keep the sand from our eyes and these humps to store water, but…Mom?"

"Yes, son? What is it this time?"

"Why the heck are we in the San Diego Zoo?"

What is the purpose of this story? Once you master all the features of Excel, and you know how to produce an excellent spreadsheet, you must be willing to show your work to its intended audience. Excel has a lot of options to help you produce output of your worksheet or make them available where they are mostly needed and useful. Some of these options include:

1. Printing your worksheet for viewing and sharing
2. Sending the worksheet as e-mail attachment
3. Making your worksheet available over the Internet

Printing your worksheet

Unlike *Microsoft Word*, Microsoft Excel provides easy access of all its print options through the Page Setup dialog box. In the Page Setup dialog box, Excel allows you to make different choices, thereby do more than adjusting the page orientation. You can set margins, headers and footers and also take advantage of other highly useful options as well. From the Page Setup, Excel will actually let you print preview your worksheet, define and control the final output before printing begins and input header and footer plus more. Snapshot of the Page Setup window is hereby presented for your convenience:

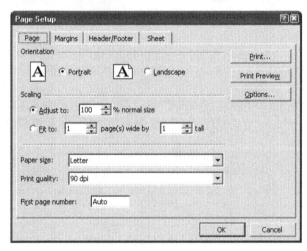

How to print Excel Worksheet with row numbers

Steps:

1. Click **File** → **Page Setup**, and then click the **Sheet** tab.

2. Under **Print**, click in the check box next to **Row and Column Headings** to select it.

3. Click **Print**.

Create Headers and Footers

A header is a piece of text (usually the title, company name or the name of the author of your worksheet) that is repeated at the top of each page. On the other hand, footer is a text that is repeated at the bottom of each page. Excel is designed to automatically produce some pre-designed headers and footers from which you can choose, or create a custom header or footer depending on your need.

1. To add a pre-designed header or footer, follow these steps:

2. Click **File** → **Page Setup** to open the *Page Setup* dialog window.

3. Click the **Header and Footer** tab to activate the following dialog window:

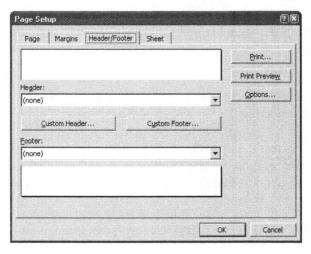

4. Click the little tinny arrow to the right of the box under **Header** (the box is currently displaying *(none)*) to pick any of the pre-designed Header from those listed

5. Do the same to select Footer

6. Click **Ok**.

Create a custom Header or Footer

1. Click **File → Page Setup** to open the page dialog window.
2. Click the **Header/Footer** tab
3. Click either the **Custom Header** or the **Custom Footer** to activate the following window

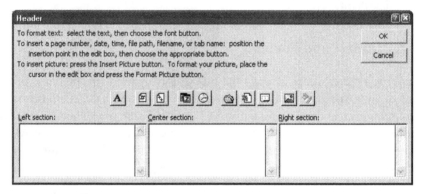

4. Click the **Left Section** to add text such as your company's name
5. Click the **Center Section** to perhaps add page number, and finally
6. Click the **Right Section** to add something like the author's name or the company address

If you are going to use the ampersand, (&), in the company's name, as in **Larry & Joe Limberg**, you must type the ampersand twice. This is highly necessary and required. It tells Excel that you intend to use the ampersand as part of your text and not trying to specify code syntax. In this case, you will type the company's name as **Larry && Joe Limberg** (no space between the two ampersands). Should you like to know more about the subject of Header and Footer in Excel, feel free to visit www.mednetservices.com from time to time for lots of Free downloads.

Print two worksheets from separate workbooks on the same page

Do you have data on two or even more Microsoft Excel worksheets that you'd like to print on a single page? If you had been wondering if this is really possible, wonders no more. I am happy to let you know that it is possible. You can actually produce a combined printout, even if the worksheets are in different workbooks. The first thing to do is open a new worksheet and create links to the two or more separate worksheet that you would like to print.

For example, let's assume you have Financial Statement on one worksheet, Balance Sheet on another and Changes in Financial Position on yet another worksheet.

Let's further assume that you plan to continue keeping the report (Financial Statement, Balance Sheet and Changes in Financial Position) and the details on their respective separate worksheets as it's currently the case. However, you want to print them all on the same page. Follow these steps:

1. Open a blank worksheet. For example, you could add a sheet to the workbook and name it Financial Report.

2. Open the Financial Statement worksheet. Click **Select All** to select the entire worksheet.

3. From the **Edit** menu, click **Copy**.

4. Go back to the new worksheet (the one you named Financial Report), click the upper-left cell of the area where you want the data to appear. For example, to place the Financial Statement at the top of the page, all you need to do is click cell **A1**.

5. On the **Edit** menu, click **Paste special**, and then click **Paste Link**. This new action would link data on the new worksheet to its original source. This is necessary and required if you want changes to the original worksheet to automatically appear on the new worksheet.

6. To format the cells on the new worksheet to match the original range of data from the data source, click **Paste special** again, and then click **Formats**.

7. Now go to the other worksheet (the Balance Sheet worksheet) containing the next range of data that you want to print on the same page. Select the exact range of data that you want to copy.

8. Go back to the new worksheet (the one you named Financial Report), click the cell where you want the data to appear.

9. From the **Edit** menu, click **Copy**. Do not forget to let the new area remain selected.

10. Go back to the **Edit** menu, click **Paste special**, and then click **Paste Link**. To copy the formatting too, click **Paste special** again, and then click **Formats**.

11. Repeat steps 7 through step 10 to copy Changes in Financial Position to the new worksheet.

Print Large Worksheet to fit one page

Depending on your data, you might want to adjust column widths or row heights. Formatting and adjustments affect only the new worksheet, and not the original worksheets that you're linking to.

1. When you've finished with the new worksheet and you are ready to print, click **File,** and then click the **Page Setup** to set any print options you want before you print the new worksheet. For example, if the new worksheet is too large but you would rather have it on one page anyway, do the following:

   a. Click the radio button next to **Landscape,** and also the radio button next to **Fit to** under *Scaling.*

   b. Make sure the **Fit to** be left at page 1 and the **page(s) wide by** is also left at 1. Depending on the size of your worksheet, Microsoft Excel would let you print on Letter size paper or Legal size paper.

2. It is advisable to use the new worksheet for printing purposes, and continue to maintain your data on the original worksheets.

3. When you open the workbook containing the new worksheet (Financial Report), make sure you update links, and the new worksheet will always reflect the latest changes to the original data in the data source.

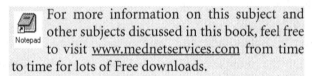

For more information on this subject and other subjects discussed in this book, feel free to visit www.mednetservices.com from time to time for lots of Free downloads.

Using standard Print dialog window

You can always use the standard **Print** dialog window to generate a hard copy of your worksheet by doing the following:

1. Click **File → Print** and this should activate the Print dialog window

2. Under *Print Range,* click **All** to print your entire workbook or select *Page range*

3. Under *Print what,* click to print the **Active Sheet(s)** or click to print the **Entire Workbook.**

4. Under *Copies,* do not forget to indicate the **Number of copies** as well as whether you want to **Collate** while printing

5. Click **Ok** to start printing.

E-Mail Attachment—Online Collaboration

We need to be mindful of the fact that the lack of face-to-face contact places a premium on sharing information efficiently. By the same token, we need to be equally mindful of the fact that it is undoubtedly easier and faster to exchange documents and other types of information nowadays than anytime in the history of human existence—thanks to the Internet.

A Loan Amortization worksheet due to be presented to the Board of Directors this afternoon in San Diego can be prepared by a Certified Public Accountant whose office is in New York, sent to the Medical Director who is attending a symposium in Singapore (and a copy sent to the Senior Vice President who is on vacation in Lagos, Nigeria) for review and approval. The same document can be sent to the Sr. Vice President who is on her way to a business conference in Geneva, Switzerland and still be made available on time in San Diego, California.

Microsoft Excel 2000 and 2002 are designed to make it easier for you to send your worksheet to any recipient for review or as an attachment to an e-mail. To send your worksheet, follow these steps:

1. When you finish preparing your worksheet, click **File → Send To.**

2. Choose **Mail Recipient (for review)…**or **Mail Recipient (as attachment)…**

3. Depending on the option of your choice, you might be asked to save your worksheet with a different name to keep track of changes made by the intending recipient.

4. The system should activate Microsoft Outlook, arrange your email with your attachment in place just like the following screen:

5. Unless you intend to add more messages, the next step should be to sup-ply the recipient e-mail address and click **Send** button on the message toolbar to send your message.

Save e-Mail Attachment

In this section, I am going to assume that your *Microsoft Outlook Express 6* is configured to send and receive e-mail messages using your existing e-mail account. If that is the case, all you need to do to save any attachment file that comes with your e-mail message is follow these steps:

1. Click the **Send/Receive** button on the Outlook Express toolbar to download all your new e-mail messages
2. Open your **e-Mails** one by one
3. When you come across the one with attachment, click on **the attachment** and you would be presented with an option to **Save Attachment.**
4. Click on it to save the attachment to the directory of your choice.

Posting your worksheet on the Internet

Every application program in Microsoft Office 2000 and Office 2002 is designed to make integration with the Web a lot easier. You can post Microsoft Excel worksheet as an interactive Web page or non interactive Web page. Any of these would probably help to increase the usefulness of the worksheet.

Web Page Preview

To preview your worksheet in a web browser without publishing it, do the following:

1. Make sure the worksheet you intend to preview is the one currently displaying on your Microsoft Excel.
2. Click **File → Web Page Preview.**
3. If after you clicked Web Page Preview and the same Excel file is still showing, go to the Status bar and look for a file opened by your Internet Explorer, and click on it.
4. Depending on the size of your worksheet, you may have to scroll to view the entire sheet.

Publish a workbook as an interactive Web page

Follow these steps:

1. Click **File → Save** to save your workbook in regular Excel format before you publish your workbook as interactive Web Page.

2. Click **File → Save as Web Page** to activate the following *Save As* dialog window

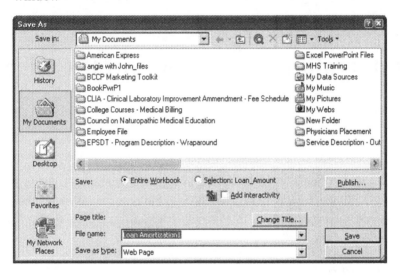

3. Click the **Save In** box to select the folder you want to publish to (this is usually a folder within your web folder).

4. Select **Entire Workbook** to publish the workbook in Web format

5. Click the check box next to **Add Interactivity.** As soon as you click this, the system would change your **File Name** to, probably a default name such as *Page.htm.* Feel free to change the name to reflect the worksheet name but do not forget to include the (**htm**) extension.

6. Click **Publish.** (This will only publish to the folder you specified in step 3 above. However, feel free to preview your interactive page in your browser before you publish your entire web page(s) to the Internet.)

A great pleasure in life is doing what
people say you cannot do.
—Walter Gagehot

CHAPTER EIGHT

Integration within Microsoft Office

The first part of this chapter is taken literally from volume one of *Beyond Cut, Copy and Paste*. After the first part which deals mainly with integration with *Microsoft Excel* from within *Microsoft Word*, I am going to show you how you can take a database developed in *Microsoft Excel* and use it in *Microsoft Word Mail Merge*.

From Word to Excel

Inability of one program to perform what other programs can do so very well is not really of a serious concern in Microsoft Office. You are well aware that there are some calculations you can perform in Microsoft Word table but on the other hand, there are a lot you wouldn't be able to do. However, if you are having problems doing those calculations in Word, you can simply walk across the isle (not literally) and bring Excel into Word and this is known as embedding. When you embed Excel worksheet into Word, you are in a way asking Excel to come into the Word suite with all its worksheets, formulas, menus and toolbars.

In this section, we are going to deal extensively with embedding Excel worksheets in Word Documents. This will lead us to do some of the complex calculations we would love to do in Word but could not do due to its limitations. The **Insert Microsoft Excel Worksheet** button ▦ on the **Standard** toolbar lets you embed Excel worksheet in Word document.

We've just been asked to send a memo to every Psychiatrist and Therapist including Case Managers to let them know that the Central Office is in the process of closing some cases. The closing is scheduled to affect patients who have not been back in the clinic within the last 60 days for whatever reasons. But before this closing, we have to inform each Psychiatrist, Therapist and Case Manager just in case they would like to contact any of those patients to inform them about the pending action of the central office.

Dealing with Memorandum

Regardless of which style you prefer, all memorandum styles contain, basically, the same elements. The lead words area is usually in double space and with the following elements:

> To:
> From:
> Date:
> Subject:

The body of the memo comes next and is usually in single space. The last part of the memo could be a Reference, or an Attachment. To fully understand this, let us reproduce the following memo:

MidMed©

To:	Psychiatrists and Therapists
From:	Clinical Director
Date:	April 8, 2004
Subject:	Administrative Discharge

Our record indicates that the following patients have been in inactive status for more than 60 days and we are about to initiate administrative discharge. I'm hereby asking you to carefully review the following list and kindly contact those that are your patients to inform them of the pending action.

cc: Vice President of Operations

Embedding Excel Worksheets in Word

1. Click to place the cursor at the location where you want to insert Excel Worksheet. In our case, we are going to insert the worksheet after the last line of the only paragraph in the Memo. At the end of "inform them of the pending action," press **Enter.**

2. Click **Insert Microsoft Excel Worksheet** button on the **Standard** toolbar.

3. Move your mouse to cover all the rows and columns and click the mouse. Expand the worksheet to accommodate five rows and six columns

4. Enter the following information:

    a. First row, **Column one** = Patient ID, **Column two** = First Name, **Column three** = Last Name, **Column four** = SS Number, **Column five** = Admission Date and **Column six** = Phone Number. Feel free to format the heading as you like.

    b. In column one of the second row, type the following formula (no space anywhere):

    =Left(B2)&Left(C2)&Right(D2,4) and press **Enter**

5. Choose **Data → Form,** and

    a. Enter the following information (without comma) beginning from the first active field: First Name = **Avon,** Last Name = **Lady,** SS Number = **021-34-9191,** Admission Date = **12/25/2002,** and Phone Number = **215-555-1212**

    b. Click **New** and enter the following two patients information (don't forget to click **New** again to enter the next information):

First Name: Sugar	Flowing
Last Name: Daddy	Alien
SS Number: 321-45-9494	645-34-9595
Admission Date: 01/21/2003	01/24/2003
Phone Number: 717-555-1212	610-555-1212

    c. Click **Close.**

6. Click **outside** of the Excel Worksheet to return to the Word mode.

When you have finished, your memo should look like this:

MidMed©

To:	Psychiatrists and Therapists
From:	Clinical Director
Date:	April 8, 2004
Subject:	Administrative Discharge

Our record indicates that the following patients have been in inactive status for more than 60 days and we are about to initiate administrative discharge. I'm hereby asking you to carefully review the following list and kindly contact those that are your patients to inform them of the pending action.

Patient ID	First Name	Last Name	SS Number	Admission Date	Phone Number
AL9191	Avon	Lady	021-34-9191	12/25/2002	215-555-1212
SD9393	Sugar	Daddy	025-51-9393	12/26/2002	610-555-1212
FA9595	Flowing	Alien	645-34-9595	1/24/2003	610-555-1212

cc: Vice President of Operations

Copy an Excel Table in Word

Another way to handle the task we just finished is to complete the worksheet in Excel and copy it into Word document. The feature for this also provides the option to have Excel retain its formatting, and also match the table style in Excel with the copy in Word document. Not only that, changes made to the original will also reflect in the copy. Unfortunately, this feature is only available in Excel XP (2002). Follow the steps outlined below to copy a table from Excel to Word:

1. Open Excel, and select the table you want to copy.
2. On the **Edit** menu, click **Copy**, or right-click on the selected table and on the pop up menu, click **Copy**
3. Open **Microsoft Word** without closing Excel, and then click where you want to insert the table.
4. Click **Edit** and then click **Paste Options**.
5. To link the table so that it automatically updates when changes are made in the source (the original Excel copy), select **Keep Source Formatting and Link to Excel**, and otherwise select **Keep Source Formatting**.

Use Microsoft Excel database in Microsoft Word Mail Merge

The quest for a better, easier and more efficient ways to do many things, thereby accomplish our objectives has led to a lot of outstanding improvement in the field of Information Technology. You don't have to rely on the *Mail Merge* tools in *Microsoft Word* to create and manage your data source exclusively. When you really look at it, the Mail Merge tool has its limitations. Let us assume that you want to create a data source to keep track of visitors to your website. Let's assume that the purpose of this data source is to be able to send mailings to those visitors, unless you make it possible to automate this tasks, you will discover that not only is the process time consuming but also very costly.

With *Microsoft Office*, you can create a database, publish it as an interactive Web page that you can use to collect whatever information from your website visitors and later use that same database as the data source for your *Mail Merge*. The following steps assume that you've created a database in Excel named Patient Registration. The database contains some important information such as Patient ID, First Name, Last Name, Address, City, State, Zip Code, Social Security Number, etc. The steps also assume that the database is fully populated with real people's information. If that is the case, let us go ahead and follow the steps as hereby outlined.

Steps

1. Start your Microsoft Word 2000
2. Open the existing document which is your letter and make sure it is showing in the active window.
3. Choose **Tools → Mail Merge** to display the Mail Merge Helper.
4. Click the **Create** button under Step 1 Main document, and then select **Form Letters**.
5. Word will give you a choice to use the **Active Window**, which is the document window that is opened behind the dialog window. Or, start a **New Main Document**, which will open a new blank document window. In this case, we are going to click the **Active Window**.
6. Word takes you back to the Mail Merge Helper dialog window, which now displays the type of merge and the name and *path* of the document under the Main Document step.
7. Choose **Get Data** under Step 2 on the Mail Merge Helper dialog window; then choose **Open Data Source** to display the Select Data Source dialog window.

8. Click in **Look in** box to select the directory where you have your Excel database file

9. Click the database file and click **Open.**

Inserting Merge Fields to your Document

Once you have completed importing of the *data source* for your mail merge from *Microsoft Excel* to *Microsoft Word*, you are ready to insert *merge fields* in the main document. Merge fields are the variable information that changes for each document. The document could be a letter, envelope, labels, form, invoice, or agreement, or any document such as a newsletter or even a brochure. In addition to your existing toolbar, you will see two new buttons. One is labeled **Insert Merge Field** and the other one is labeled **Insert Word Field**

Steps

1. Make sure the main document is still open.

2. Position the insertion point where you want a merge field to appear.

3. Click the **Insert Merge Field** button on the Mail Merge toolbar, and then select the field of choice from the list presented.

4. Repeat step 3 above until all your intended fields are inserted in their appropriate places. For further help, go to paragraph three which is page 16 through to page 24 of **Volume One.**

CHAPTER NINE

The Next Step

Maria	Hey, Doc.! This is really great.
HB	What are you talking about, Maria?
Maria	I'm talking about the subjects you covered here with this explanation of Excel—you really went deep. The way you kind of break each topic down to steps anyone could understand regardless of their background. You genuinely made working with numbers something to enjoy.
HB	Thanks. That means a lot to me.
Maria	May I ask you a question?
HB	Sure. What is it?
Maria	You are so good in this stuff doc! The way you explains it, your sense of humor, your patience and how you do everything with such a big smile on your face all the time! It's amazing! How long did it take you to know all these stuff and be as good and as comfortable as you are now?
HB	Wow! Thank you very much Maria. Well, I am going to answer your question with a story I first came across in the December 1989 issue of *Bits and Pieces*. I've also seen the same story in different publications after that.
Maria	It must be a very good story!
HB	Indeed it is! "Some years ago, a successful businessman was attending a conference on the role of business in society. He was a hardworking, self-made man whose rough-hewn exterior belied the depth of his wisdom and common sense about life."

Maria	That reminds me of my dad
HB	Is that right? "Suddenly, without warning and near the end of the conference, he was called upon to speak to the group—leading businessmen from all over the country—a powerful, famous, sophisticated audience. He rose and made his way uncertainly to the platform. As he began to speak, his words were hesitant, and his voice faltered."
Maria	Oh my God!
HB	"Gradually, however, he began to speak from the depths of his experience. As he spoke about those things closest to his heart, the words and thoughts came. He delivered a powerful, profoundly moving speech. And when he had finished, the room broke into spontaneous applause—he was given a standing ovation."
Maria	Wow! That's great!
HB	"Later, at an informal gathering, a cocky, ingratiating young executive complimented him. 'That was some speech,' he said. 'How long did it take you to write it?' The older man looked gently at the younger one for a moment, then said, 'About 60 years, young man, about 60 years!'"
Maria	You are so deep! I…I don't know…You are just amazing! Would you mind to join me tonight for dinner?
HB	I hope you wouldn't mind a rain check on that one!
Maria	Hey, what can I say? (Maria giggles) Rain Check! What is that anyway? Isn't that like putting someone on hold!
HB	I don't know! To me, it sounds like "I would love to but let me finish what I'm doing right now."
Maria	That's cool! I seriously don't mind doc! I'll see you tomorrow for the next project and that is *Beyond e-Mail*, right?
HB	Right. Drive carefully!
Maria	I will doc! Goodnight!

ABOUT THE AUTHOR

An experienced psychotherapist, healthcare administrator, IT Professional and Author of books on computer applications and College Teacher; Dr. Balogun was a Small Business Development (SBD) consultant for Bryant College, Community College of Rhode Island and Salve Regina University. He was the President and CEO of Hengrab Medical when he received the Distinguished Leadership Award for Outstanding Service to the Health Care Profession. He is currently the CEO of MedNet Healthcare Systems an acclaimed healthcare/IT consultant. He recently resumes teaching at the Bucks County Community College in the Nursing & Allied Health department—one of the subjects he is appointed to teach include Microsoft Office for Healthcare Professionals.

INDEX

0-595-31669-7